Macaulay Culkin

RichieRich

A NOVELIZATION BY JORDAN HOROWITZ
BASED ON THE SCREENPLAY WRITTEN BY
TOM S. PARKER & JIM JENNEWEIN

FAMILY ENTERTAINMENT

READING

SCHOLASTIC INC.

New York Toronto London Auckland Sydney

ISBN 0-590-25086-8

Designed by N.L. Kipnis

12 11 10 9 8 7 6 5 4 3 2 1   4 5 6 7 8 9/9

Printed in the U.S.A.   01

First Scholastic printing, December 1994

Chapter 1

The private helicopter swooped over the top of the United Tool Company factory building and hovered there for a moment. It glistened against the deep blue sky like a jewel. Its whirling rotor blades were made of pure gold. So were its body and the bolts that held it together. Emblazoned just beneath the tail rotor were the initials R.R.

From his seat inside the cockpit twelve-year-old Richie Rich watched as a crowd of workers and their families gathered on the lawn below to meet the helicopter. Many television news reporters were also there with cameras and microphones. All watched as the helicopter slowly began to descend, its rotors creating a great whirlwind that flattened the grass below it into a wide landing pad.

As soon as the helicopter landed the crowd of workers rushed up to it. They were a mix of modestly dressed men and women who had spent most of their lives working for the United Tool Company. Once the great company had provided them with income and benefits, enough to feed them when they were hungry and care for them when they were sick. But times had changed. Computers and robotics had made other companies more efficient. The United Tool Company was soon not making enough money to stay in business. Its owners were going to close shop and fire its more than six hundred employees. That's when Richie's dad, Richard Rich, stepped in. Legendary in the business world as a man who put people before profits, Mr. Rich bought the United Tool Company and saved it from bankruptcy. In doing so he also hoped to save the jobs of everyone who was now clamoring around the helicopter. Each and every one of the workers was grateful. Each and every one wanted to thank Mr. Rich personally. That's why they were there waiting eagerly for the billionaire to arrive. They had arranged a presentation in his honor. Now they were all hoping to catch the first glimpse of the famous man who had saved their jobs.

Richie pulled at the collar of his white button-down shirt. He was dressed in his usual custom-tailored three-piece suit, but today he felt uncomfortable. His dad had been called out of town on business. That meant that Richie had to stand in for him at the presentation. Normally that was no problem for Richie. He had been taught since birth that he was special. That he was different from the other kids. Being the son of a billionaire carried with it certain privileges, but it also carried certain responsibilities. Among them making appearances for the public and the press.

But when the helicopter first approached the factory, Richie glimpsed a group of kids far across the lawn. Richie knew they were probably the children of the factory workers. They had started up a game of softball. Despite their inexpensive blue jeans and worn sneakers, the kids looked like they were having fun. Richie realized that he had never played a game of softball with kids his own age. He may have had season tickets to every baseball game in the country, complete with a reserved seat right behind the dugout, but that wasn't the same.

Suddenly Richie wished that he didn't have to act so grown-up all the time. He wished he could be a normal kid.

Richie Rich was twelve years old, but today he felt more like thirty.

The helicopter blades finally came to a stop and the pilot opened the cockpit door. A short staircase descended to the ground.

Richie watched as the workers and reporters peered over each other trying to get a look inside. Richie felt like a fish in a fishbowl.

Then Richie looked to either side of him. He had been sandwiched between two men since the trip began. He knew the routine. He would have to wait for their signal before he could leave the helicopter.

The first man was Ferguson, the head security guard. Ferguson was a huge brawny man dressed in a dark suit and sunglasses. Richie didn't like him very much. He looked like a member of the Secret Service. Richie waited as Ferguson climbed out of the helicopter, pushed some of the workers and reporters aside, and made sure that the immediate area around the helicopter was cleared.

Richie looked to his left at the other man. This was Richie's personal valet, Herbert Arthur Runcible Cadbury. Richie liked Cadbury very much. In fact, Cadbury was the closest thing Richie had to a real friend despite the vast difference in their ages.

Cadbury patted Richie on the shoulder, then climbed out of the cockpit. He was very tall and stood as straight as a telephone pole. As soon as he reached the ground, he remained at attention at the foot of the stairs.

Then a hush fell over the crowd. Richie could see the news photographers readying their cameras. It was time. He climbed out of the cockpit.

"Hi," Richie said to everyone. "My dad couldn't make it, so he sent me. I'm Richie."

There was a moment of confused silence. After all, everybody was expecting to see a much older Richard Rich. But the sight of Richie was too charming to resist. The news people began snapping his picture. One of the workers walked right up to him and shook his hand.

"Welcome to United Tool, Richie," said the worker. "My name's Dave Walter. I'm the manager of the plant. And this is Diane

Koscinski, our union rep. She'll be making the presentation for us today."

Diane Koscinski stepped forward and shook Richie's hand, too. She was an attractive woman in her middle thirties who wore bright colors and a set of big, flashy bracelets that rattled when she moved her arms.

"We're so glad you could come," Diane said to the little billionaire. "Me, too. Big thrill," replied Richie without enthusiasm. Through the crowd he was still able to catch a glimpse of the kids playing softball. "This is Cadbury."

Cadbury stepped forward. "Master Richie's personal valet," he explained.

"A valet, huh?" asked Diane. "I never met one of your type."

Diane held out her hand and offered Cadbury a handshake.

Cadbury refused to shake hands. "That does not surprise me, madam," he said bowing stiffly. Cadbury was a bit of a snob.

Diane decided to ignore Cadbury's insulting remark. This was a day to be gracious. So she politely led Richie and his valet to a microphone that had been set up a few feet away.

"Fellow workers," Diane said into the microphone. "It's not just this company that owes Mr. Rich its thanks, but this whole town. So to mark this special morning, the first day of the retooling that's gonna bring our jobs back, we're gonna ask Richie to accept this token of our appreciation for his dad."

As the crowd applauded, a little seven-year-old girl stepped forward and presented Richie with a set of gold-plated socket wrenches on a satin pillow.

But Richie wasn't looking at the gift. Instead, his attention was still riveted on the kids playing in the field. Suddenly he felt a push from behind. It was Cadbury nudging him to accept the golden wrenches.

"On behalf of my dad," said Richie as he

took the satin pillow, "thanks for the wrenches. I know my dad loves socket wrenches. I know I love socket wrenches. And if my mom ever knew what a socket wrench was, I'm sure she'd love them, too. I'd like to stay, but I gotta go do my homework. It's been real."

Then Richie quickly slipped through the crowd and ran to a fence. On the other side of the fence were the kids who had been playing softball. A girl was pitching and she had just struck out the boy who was at bat.

Richie smiled. He wished he could climb over the fence and play with the kids. Just then he felt someone grab him from behind. It was Ferguson.

"This area is not secure, sir," said Ferguson. "Please return to the helicopter immediately."

"But I just wanted to — " explained Richie.

"I said return to the helicopter!" repeated Ferguson firmly. His grip was getting harder.

"Don't touch him!" came Cadbury's voice from behind. Ferguson released Richie when he saw Cadbury approach.

"Master Richie," said Cadbury. "We must be on our way. You have a very busy afternoon."

Richie looked longingly at the kids in the field. Then he turned and walked back toward the helicopter.

When he was several feet away, Cadbury and Ferguson exchanged angry looks, each man resenting the other.

"It's my job to protect him," explained Ferguson in a firm voice.

"Very well," agreed Cadbury. "But grab him like that again and *you* will need protection."

Then Cadbury turned stiffly and walked away.

Ferguson tightened his lips into a sneer as he watched Cadbury catch up with Richie. This wasn't the first time he and the valet locked horns over the boy and he knew it wouldn't be the last.

Once inside the helicopter, Richie continued to look toward the kids playing ball.

"I wonder what it's like, Cadbury," he began longingly, "to be like them."

Cadbury said nothing. Instead, he thought back over the years to that cold and frosty November day when Richie was born. From that moment on Cadbury, who had been the Rich family butler, became Richie's personal valet.

Over the years he watched Richie grow into a handsome, intelligent young man who soon became used to nothing but the best. He remembered Richie as a newborn infant laying in his 24-karat gold crib. Hanging over the crib was a mobile of animals made out of international currency. At five years old Richie was driving his kiddie car in and out of the 250 rooms of the Rich mansion. The car was made by Mercedes, of course, and it was loaded with every luxury known to a five year old. Then, at ten, Richie was able to practice baseball with Reggie Jackson as his personal coach.

But now Cadbury sensed that Richie, at twelve, seemed sadder than he ever had been before. It was as if the boy knew that there was something missing in his life. Something money could not buy.

Cadbury was deep in thought as the helicopter approached the front lawn of Rich Manor.

Chapter 2

The Rich estate was a sprawling 957-acre stretch of beautiful countryside, flowing waterfalls, forests, and rolling hills. It was, according to *Fortune* magazine, one of the largest and most valuable estates in the entire world.

No sooner had the helicopter entered the estate boundaries than the telephone rang. Cadbury reached over and picked up the receiver. It was Richie's mother and she had good news.

"Master Rich," said Cadbury as he hung up the phone. "Your father is home from his business trip."

Richie's face brightened. His solemn gaze gave way to a broad smile. It was the first time he had smiled all day.

Moments later the helicopter set down on the lawn of Rich Manor. The manor was designed like a French chateau, a combination of mansion and country house. And it was big, looming tall and wide across the great lawn, one end never visible from the other. Behind the mansion was a large swimming pool in the shape of a dollar sign, and a race track where Richie drove miniature cars. Then there was the tennis court, the riding stable, and the roller coaster.

Richie burst out of the golden helicopter even before its blades stopped spinning. He raced across the lawn and up the many steps that led to the huge front doors of the house. Richie pulled the doors open and ran inside. Cadbury was hurrying to catch up.

Dollar, Richie's pedigreed Jack Russell terrier, ran across the marble foyer to meet his master.

"Hey, Dollar!" said Richie. "Where're Mom

14

and Dad?" Dollar barked and then trotted off past the rows of priceless paintings and statues that adorned the foyer. Richie removed his jacket and tossed it over the arm of one of the Roman statues. Then he loosened his tie and followed his dog.

With an awestruck expression, Richard Rich looked out of the large picture window in the living room. He was a tall, broad man with shortly cut light brown hair and an expressive face that never hid his true feelings. What he was feeling now was astonishment. Far in the distance, atop one of the rolling hills of the estate, a construction crew was busy. They were chiseling the faces of Richie and Mr. and Mrs. Rich into the side of one of the hills.

Mrs. Rich called it Mount Richmore.

"I said we should have a family portrait, Regina," said Mr. Rich. "But this?"

Mrs. Rich stopped trimming the flowers she was readying for a vase and walked up beside her husband. She, too, had a broad figure, but a gentle, delicate face.

"Sweetheart," she explained to her husband. "It wasn't my idea. It was the artist who came up with it. And who are we to stifle her creativity."

"How'd she do it so fast?" asked Mr. Rich. "I've only been gone for a week."

Mrs. Rich smiled. "Professor Keenbean invented some sort of photon … particle … maximizer. Something like that," she said, trying to explain. "Seems to do the job."

"Honey, you know me," said Mr. Rich. "I'm all for the arts, but isn't this a tad pretentious? Our faces a hundred feet high? Wait'll Geraldo gets ahold of this."

"Oh, Richard," Mrs. Rich sighed. "You're overreacting. Or is there something about it you don't like?"

"Well," began Mr. Rich as he pointed to the huge bust of himself that stared back at him from across the estate. "My cheeks are too puffy. I know I've put on a few pounds, Regina, but you have to admit, I do loom puffy up there."

Just then Richie burst into the living room.

"Dad! You're home!" he shouted happily and jumped into the warm, waiting arms of his father.

"Hey, slugger," said Mr. Rich with a hug. "Great to see you!"

Next Richie hugged his mother and let her kiss him on the cheek.

"How was the ribbon cutting at United Tool?" asked Mrs. Rich.

"Terrific," Richie answered. "They gave Dad a gift."

Cadbury had quietly followed Richie into the living room. In his hand was the red satin pillow and the golden wrenches.

"Socket wrenches, sir," said Cadbury. He presented the gift to Mr. Rich.

"Socket wrenches!" Mr. Rich exclaimed his eyes widening ardently. "I love socket wrenches."

"And Dad," added Richie. "While I was there I saw these kids playing and — "

"Excuse me, sir," interrupted Cadbury. "There is a telephone call in your study. The President."

"Of what country?" asked Mr. Rich.

"Ours, sir."

Mr. Rich winced. "Probably needs another loan," he said. "I'll just be a minute."

Mr. Rich walked out of the living room.

Richie's smile dropped. He wanted so desperately to tell his father about the kids he saw playing in the United Tool Company field. Now he would have to wait. As usual, business came first in the Rich household.

Suddenly Richie had a great idea. He could invite the kids from the United Tool Company field to his house for a game of softball. That way he would be able to play with them.

"Mom," said Richie. "I was wondering, if it's okay with you, can I invite some kids over?"

"Of course, dear," said Mrs. Rich. She was thrilled at the idea. "A dinner party. Just tell me how many and when and we'll send out the invitations."

"Not a party, Mom. Just something — "

"Informal? All right. More like a buffet.

We'll have it in the Oak Room. That should be large enough to accommodate your friends from school."

"My friends from school?" asked Richie. "They're always too busy to come over. So I thought — "

BEEP! BEEP! BEEP! Suddenly an alarm sounded from Cadbury's pocket. He pulled out his pocket organizer and flipped it open.

"Master Richie," he said. "Time for your chemistry lesson with Professor Keenbean."

Richie frowned. "Do I have to?" he asked. "We must keep to our schedule, sir," replied Cadbury.

So much for his great idea. He followed Cadbury out of the room.

After Richie had gone, Mrs. Rich stood at the living room window and dialed the telephone. A moment later Raphaella, the artist, answered. Mrs. Rich explained that her husband thought the sculptors were making his cheeks a little too full.

"He says they're a little puffy," explained Mrs. Rich into the phone. "I was wondering if maybe you could do something — anything. A little liposuction perhaps? Thank you ever so much."

No sooner had she hung up the phone than she saw the sculptors go to work on the hilltop. Lasers blasted. Sanders sanded. Mr. Rich's cheeks became thinner in seconds.

Just then Mr. Rich returned.

"I'm afraid I've got some bad news, honey," he told his wife carefully.

"Don't tell me," said Mrs. Rich. "You're flying out again."

"Tonight after dinner," confirmed Mr. Rich. "I'm sorry."

"You just got in. We were supposed to spend some time together."

Mr. Rich walked over to his wife and gently embraced her. It was true, he was called away on business too often. He knew it was an imposition on his family, but he hoped they knew he was doing it all for them.

"How do you put up with me?" he asked his wife.

"Well, you do have seventy million dollars," replied Mrs. Rich.

"Is that the only reason?" Mr. Rich knew it wasn't.

"You also have a nice butt," added Mrs. Rich playfully. Then she kissed her husband and scooted out of the living room, passing Cadbury on the way.

Mr. Rich glowed. He walked over to a mirror and looked at his behind. Mrs. Rich was right. It was a nice butt.

"Did you hear that, Cadbury?" asked Mr. Rich as he swerved his behind from side to side for a better view.

"Indeed, sir," said Cadbury with a smile.

"Madam admires your butt. I am most delighted for you."

Mr. Rich smiled happily. It had taken him a long time to find the kind of woman that he would want to marry. He knew early on that it would have to be someone who wouldn't marry him just because of his money. Regina was such a woman.

Then his smile changed to a frown. It was true; he had married the perfect woman. Not only that, Richie was the best son a man could want. He always noticed the hurt expressions on their faces when he was called out of town. Lately he had seen those expressions more frequently.

After this trip, he decided, he would have to change all that.

Chapter 3

In a laboratory in the basement of Rich Manor Professor Keenbean stood in front of his latest invention. It was a huge device. A large bucket, at least eight feet across, was moving down a long conveyor toward a Dumpster-sized vat.

The Professor was a chubby man whose belly challenged the buttons on his white coat. His frizzy hair stuck out from his head and he wore thick, bottle-like black frame glasses. He was always eating and his lab coat had the spots to prove it.

At the same time, Keenbean looked

straight into a video camera that was being operated by his lab assistant. He was in the middle of a special demonstration.

"You stockholders are now looking at the twenty-first century's answer to the problem of waste management," Keenbean said to the camera. "Our newest invention: The Subatomic Molecular Reorganizer!"

The bucket came to a stop over the vat and the bucket's hinged bottom creaked open. A variety of items such as old tires, aluminum cans, plastic milk cartons, and food scraps plummeted into the vat. Suddenly the vat came to life with a series of mechanical whirrs and hisses. Steam rose up through the fiery white light coming from the machine.

Professor Keenbean strapped a pair of protective goggles over his eyes and started punching some of the appropriate keys on the reorganizer's keypad. The sounds from the vat became louder and it began to vibrate intensely.

"Useless garbage is quickly broken down

into basic molecular components," he explained to the camera. "Then they are recombined to form a whole range of useful products from bedpans to bowling balls. Hey, need a new bedpan? I sure do."

He punched the word BEDPAN into the keypad. Then he walked over to one end of the machine and stopped at a little door and waited patiently for his bedpan to push through.

"It's quick," he said as he waited. "It's easy. In no time at all we've turned fifteen pounds of yesterday's trash into a beautiful — "

Just then the little door opened and something slid through. Only it wasn't a bedpan. It was a bowling ball.

" — a bowling ball?" Keenbean said, his face turning red with embarrassment. He quickly tried to cover his mistake. "A thoroughly useful bowling ball," he continued as he placed his fingers into the three holes of the ball. He tried lifting the ball, but it was too heavy. No matter how hard he tried, the ball wouldn't budge. He leaned over the ball and pushed with his shoulders, his stomach, his legs. Anything that would help. The ball finally inched off the table and plummeted to the floor, shattering into a thousand tiny bits.

He turned to the cameraman in frustration "All right, cut!" he shouted to his assistant. "Cut! Cut!"

Keenbean's assistant quickly turned off the video camera. Then he nodded and scurried off to his lab desk.

Richie had been watching from the lab doorway. He walked over to the molecular reorganizer and looked at the shattered bowling ball.

"Still not working, is it, Professor?" he asked.

"Just a few kinks still need ironing out," replied Keenbean with a red face. "Not to worry."

And with that Keenbean took Richie by the arm and led him through the lab.

"Ready for your chemistry tutorial?" he asked the boy.

"I'm kinda not in the mood, Professor," said Richie with a shrug. "What else are you working on?"

Keenbean picked up a half-eaten liverwurst sandwich and steered Richie to an area where several different scientists were hunched over various experiments. Two of them had spread rubbery black goop against the lab wall. Attached to the wall was a television set, a chair, and a two hundred-pound bowling ball.

"A new adhesive," Keenbean explained through a mouthful of liverwurst as they neared the wall. "A hundred times stickier than the strongest adhesive known to man. I call it Cementia. Oh, wait till you see what's over here!"

The Professor gestured wildly with his arm and accidentally knocked one of the scientists into the black goop on the wall.

"Help!" the poor man shouted as other scientists tried to pry him off the wall.

Then Keenbean guided Richie to another area where a male department store mannequin stood dressed in a suit. Keenbean picked up a spray bottle that was labeled Stain-Away from a nearby table.

"Now this could be the biggest thing since your father and I invented the microchip and the ice-cream sandwich."

Keenbean aimed the spray bottle at the mannequin and squeezed its handle. A colorless spray shot out onto the front of the mannequin's suit.

"Makes any fabric instantly impervious," continued Keenbean. "Dirtproof, stainproof, waterproof."

The professor then motioned to one of the other scientists. The scientist stepped forward with a rifle and aimed it at the mannequin. Then he fired a shot dead center.

Keenbean walked over to the mannequin and removed the bullet. It had been lodged in the mannequin's suit which had become metalized by the Stain-Away.

"And bulletproof," he said proudly displaying the bullet. "Works perfect every time!"

Just then the front of the suit, so hardened by the spray, ripped away from the rest and crashed to the floor like a cast-iron frying pan.

Keenbean's face turned red. "Except for one small side effect," he mumbled. "Not only does the fabric act like a suit of armor, but it weighs about the same as well."

By now Richie had moved to another experiment. On a table lay a small glass box with a bee inside it.

"What's this?" asked Richie. "A bee?"

"Not just a bee," said Keenbean proudly opening the small box. "I call it Robo-bee." Then he activated a control box complete with buttons and toggle switch. Suddenly the bee came to life with a loud buzz. It flew out of the box and hovered over Richie's head.

"Emits pheromones that attract real honeybees that follow our little guy right to the field a farmer wants pollinated," explained the professor. "Take it for a test ride."

Richie took the control box and worked the toggle. The bee buzzed and zigzagged to each of his commands.

"Teams of scientists worked night and day for five years perfecting the latest in micro-circuit technology. Millions and millions of dollars were spent on this one bee alone."

Just then Cadbury entered the laboratory carrying a tray with cups and a teapot. He placed the tray on one of the experiment tables.

"Your afternoon tea, Master Richie," Cadbury announced.

Cadbury's ears quickly picked up the faint buzzing sound in the air. Then his eye instantly caught sight of the bee. Cadbury hated to see anything untidy in the Rich household. He particularly didn't like to see bugs flying about inside the house. He immediately picked up a magazine from the table and rolled it up. Then he smashed the bee against the table with one fell swoop. After that he neatly unrolled the magazine, cleared his throat, turned sharply on his heels, and left the room.

Richie and the professor stared down at the mangled bee with their mouths agape. "I don't believe it!" Professor Keenbean cried.

Later that night Laurence Van Dough sat in the back of the limousine and grumbled unhappily to himself. He was on the way to have dinner at the home of his business partner Richard Rich and wasn't looking forward to it. For months he had been trying to stop Rich from giving so much of the corporation's money to charity, but with little success. Van Dough knew that the less money given to charity, the more the chief executives of the company could take home.

Unfortunately Richard Rich didn't see things that way. So as the limousine passed through the huge gates that led to the Rich estate, Van Dough continued grumbling to himself. The dinner would be polite enough, he knew. But he also knew that he would bring up the subject of redirecting profits. That he would plead with Mr. Rich to stop giving so much of them away. And that Mr. Rich would remain steadfast and refuse.

The sleek limousine pulled up in front of Rich Manor and came to a stop. The chauffeur stepped out and hurried around to open the back door. Van Dough, elegantly dressed in a tuxedo, stepped out and landed his foot in a mud puddle.

Van Dough looked down. His expensive Bostonian tassel loafers were covered with mud.

"Thirty-six and a half miles of driveway and you park in the five feet with a puddle," he said to the chauffeur.

"I'm very sorry, sir," said the chauffeur lowering his head.

"Sorry doesn't cut it," said Van Dough curtly. "After tonight, find another job."

Van Dough abruptly pulled his foot out of the puddle and walked toward the steps of the house. He paused there, took out his handkerchief, and began wiping the dirt from his shoes. As he did this, Ferguson emerged from the house and approached him.

"Good evening, Mr. Van Dough. So nice to see you," said Ferguson so loud that the Riches could hear him in the house. He wanted everything to appear outwardly normal. Then he leaned over and whispered into Van Dough's ear. "I checked their schedule," he said. "I got the perfect time for us to do it."

Van Dough threw Ferguson a sharp look. "Not here, you moron," he whispered back. "We'll talk later."

Van Dough quickly moved away from Ferguson and went into the house. He had been invited to dinner. And no matter how humiliating he found that to be, he did not want to give away that he was hatching a secret plan that would destroy Richard Rich forever.

Chapter 4

Richie sat at one end of the long banquet table eating his dinner. He wasn't very hungry so what he didn't eat he passed underneath his chair to Dollar. Dollar was always hungry.

Then the telephone rang. The one that was sitting next to his plate and water glass. Richie picked up the receiver.

"Hello?" he asked.

"Richie, dear," his mother's voice came through the earpiece. "Are you sure you don't want to eat with us?"

Richie looked up at the other end of the

table, where his mother, his father, and Mr. Van Dough were clustered together eating their dinner. They looked tiny to him, but that was because the Rich dinner table was nearly half a block long. The dining room was as large as a train station.

"It's okay, Mom," Richie replied to his mother. "I don't like that guy." He was looking straight at Mr. Van Dough.

"Well, neither do I," said Richie's mom into the phone that she kept next to her plate. Then she smiled politely at Van Dough, certain that he had no idea what she was talking about. "But foie de veau is very good for you."

"So tasty, too," Richie said flatly. That's when he slipped another slice of liver down to Dollar.

At the other end of the table Van Dough swallowed his vegetables. "Have I mentioned this terrine is just superb," he told Mrs. Rich. "And to combine it with this picante sauce…"

Mrs. Rich was not taken in by Van Dough's

phony flattery. "Well, I'll let the cook know," was all she could say.

"Laurence," interrupted Mr. Rich. "Can we get back to what you were saying about charitable contributions?"

Van Dough quickly changed to a more serious tone of voice. "Sir, he began. "You know I am all in favor of charity, but your donations are costing the corporation over a billion dollars a year. I just think it's time we asked ourselves: What're we getting for that?"

Mrs. Rich was stunned. "What are we getting for that?" she snapped. We are getting food banks and medical clinics, and shelters for the homeless and — "

"Which is why I also oppose this United Tool acquisition," insisted Van Dough. "We should be getting rid of deadweight like that instead of acquiring it."

"I totally agree," said Mr. Rich. "That's why I am getting rid of United Tool."

Mrs. Rich threw a shocked look at her husband. "Richard, what are you saying?" she asked with disappointment. "All those people. All those jobs."

"Brilliant, sir!" exclaimed Van Dough, a big smile stretching across his face. "Why didn't I think of that? We buy the property in bankruptcy, level the factory, subdivide and — "

"No, Laurence," Mr. Rich corrected. "I'm keeping the factory open like I said."

"Ah, yes," said Van Dough. "We bust the union, slash benefits, then sell the company?"

But Van Dough realized that he was wrong. Mr. Rich was not nodding his head in agreement.

"We don't sell the company?" Van Dough asked.

"No," said Mr. Rich. "We give it away."

"Give it away! Yes!" nodded Van Dough. Then he thought about it. "We give it away?"

"Absolutely," replied Mr. Rich. And he was dead serious, too. "We retool, modernize, then we turn control of the factory over to the workers. They know the business better than we do. Let them run it."

Mrs. Rich was smiling. "Richard, that's a wonderful plan," she said, proud of her husband.

Laurence swallowed and tried to hide his disappointment. After all, Mr. Rich still was his boss.

"Yes," he said flatly. "Wonderful."

Suddenly the dining-room doors burst open and Professor Keenbean ran in, a box cradled in his arms.

"Mr. Rich!" Keenbean exclaimed breathlessly. "I've done it! May I present the Smellmaster!" Then he eyed the food on the table. "Oh, you're dining."

But to Keenbean's surprise, Mr. Rich jumped up excitedly. "Fantastic, Keenbean!" he said. "Look at this, Regina. We've got eyeglasses to see better, hearing aids to hear better. Why not something so we can smell better?"

We do," said Mrs. Rich with a smile. "It's called Chanel."

Mr. Rich gestured to Keenbean to continue. Keenbean opened the box and pulled out a device that looked like a ray gun from a 1930's science fiction movie.

Curious, Richie walked the half-block distance and joined the others.

"Behold," said Mr. Rich as he pointed to the gun. "The Smellmaster Nine Thousand. This baby converts any smell into a digital-audio signal. Here, Rich, you do the honors."

Richie took the Smellmaster in his hands. Cool. He felt like Luke Skywalker. He pointed it toward a goblet of wine.

The Smellmaster clicked alive. "Wine," it said in a computerized voice. "Petit Sirah, 1974."

Richie grinned, enchanted. He pointed the gun at a huge floral arrangement that sat in the middle of the dining table.

"Roses," said the Smellmaster. "Hilversum demi-bloom. Fresh cut."

"Keenbean, that's marvelous," said Mrs. Rich.

Then Richie aimed the Smellmaster at Dollar, who had trotted over to join the humans.

"Calves' liver," said the gun. Richie quickly aimed the gun away from Dollar. But by then it was too late. His mother was already throwing him a suspicious look.

"Uh, better make some adjustments, Dad," Richie said handing the gun back to his father. "This thing's way out of whack. Can I be excused?"

And with that Richie quickly darted out of the room before either one of his parents could say a word.

Van Dough pointed at the Smellmaster. "This is exactly what I was talking about," he told Mr. Rich. "Toys such as these — "

"Toys?!" Mr. Rich shot back sharply. "Good heavens, man, this may be just a toy to you, but to me, it represents good old-fashioned know-how and ingenuity. And Professor Keenbean here, he's the prime example of the pioneering spirit which made this country what it is today!"

Everyone looked over at the great Professor Keenbean, who had seated himself at the dinner table and started to stuff his mouth with food. He looked up and smiled... with a roll in his mouth.

After dinner the Riches and Van Dough retired to the living room for drinks. Van Dough decided not to bring up any talk of business. The conversation at dinner had only confirmed his belief that Richard Rich and he did not see eye to eye on how the corporation should be run.

After drinks it was time for Van Dough to go. Mr. and Mrs. Rich escorted him to the front door.

"Well, I see you've added a Monet," Van Dough commented as they walked past a painting which was hanging on the wall. "And I must say, if I were you, I'd beef up the security system around here."

"Oh, I don't think that's necessary, Laurence," said Mr. Rich, smiling. "After all, our real valuables are stored in the Rich family vault."

"The vault, yes," said Van Dough, keenly interested. "You know I'd love to see that."

"Someday I'll take you on a tour," offered Mr. Rich as they approached the front door and shook hands good night.

"I'd like that," Van Dough said. He could hardly contain his excitement. The Rich family vault. The treasures must be incredible!

Van Dough left. Mrs. Rich watched him climb into his limousine and be driven away. Then she closed the door.

"I don't trust him, Richard," Mrs. Rich said warily.

"Laurence isn't so bad," Mr. Rich insisted. "A little overzealous at times, but — "

"Well, call it woman's intuition," said Mrs. Rich. "But just watch your back."

Mr. Rich felt uneasy. He knew his wife had good instincts. And if she didn't trust somebody, there was probably a good reason why that person should not be trusted.

He would, as his wife had suggested, watch his back.

Chapter 5

"Rise and shine, Master Rich. Let's not keep your personal trainer waiting."

Richie opened one eye. Then the other. Soon Cadbury's face came into focus. The valet was hovering over him trying to get him out of bed. It was 7:30 in the morning.

"Tell Arnold I don't feel like exercising this morning," groaned Richie. It didn't matter that Arnold was an international weight-lifting champion and movie star. He turned over and buried his face in his silk embroidered pillowcase.

Just then the bedroom door opened and a

beautiful young woman stepped in. She was dressed in skin-tight spandex workout pants, sneakers, and a tank top.

"Hope you don't mind," said the woman. "But Arnold cancelled. I'll be filling in today."

Richie turned over and looked at his new aerobics teacher. She was so beautiful that his eyes nearly bulged out of his head.

"Fire Arnold," Richie ordered Cadbury as he jumped out of bed and began to slip into his sweat gear.

After his workout Richie sat on the balcony outside his room and flipped through the morning paper, stopping when he came to the comics page. Lying at his feet was Dollar.

Baines, a house servant, rolled a cart with several different bowls of cereal on it out onto the balcony.

"How's the oatmeal this morning, Baines?" asked Richie as he struggled to make a choice for breakfast.

"A tad on the lumpy side, sir," replied Baines.

"Better go with Cap'n Crunch," said Richie. He took a bowl of the crispy gold-colored cereal.

"Excellent choice," said Baines. Then Baines slipped a silver tray off the cart and knelt down. He removed the cover of the tray and presented Dollar with a choice of several different bowls of dog biscuits. Dollar sniffed each one meticulously. Then he grabbed one in his teeth and trotted off to eat it.

After breakfast Richie got dressed for school. Cadbury had laid out three different suits for him on his bed. One gray, one blue, one brown. Each had the crest of Richie's school, Mt. Exeter Academy, sewn onto the breast pocket of the blazers.

He quickly picked up the blue suit and put it on. When he was nearly dressed, he stepped in front of his full-length mirror and began to tie his tie. That's when he noticed it.

There was a faint red pimple on his cheek.

"Computer," said Richie. "Locate Dad."

Something whirred inside the wall on the

other side of the room. The surface of the wall opened up and a sleek, ultramodern computer screen and keyboard rose up. It had been activated by Richie's voice.

"Data restricted," said the computer. "Enter secret password."

Richie walked over to the desk and punched the letters S-L-U-G-G-E-R into the keypad.

"Access approved," said the computer. "Locating Father now."

Hundreds of miles away, in Washington, DC, Mr. Rich was sitting in the Oval Office of the White House talking with the President of the United States.

All of a sudden a beep sounded from his breast pocket.

"Excuse me, Mr. President," said Mr. Rich. "Call on Dadlink."

"Dadlink?" the President asked with curiosity.

"My personal communications link with my son," explained Mr. Rich to the Commander in Chief. "A prototype my people have been working on. Works via satellite."

Mr. Rich pulled a wallet-sized cellular phone out of his breast pocket and flipped it open. "Richie, what is it?" he asked into the Dadlink.

Richie's face appeared on a tiny screen on the phone.

"Hi, Dad," he said. "What'cha doing?"

"I'm discussing economic policy with the President," explained his father. "Is this something important?"

"Yeah," said Richie. "I think I'm getting a zit. My first one, but I'm not sure."

Mr. Rich glanced up at the President with embarrassment.

"Richie, can we talk about this later?" he asked his son. Richie got the idea. "Okay, Dad," he said. "See you tonight. 'Bye."

Richie watched the image of his father fade from his computer screen. Then he turned around to see that Cadbury had entered his room.

"The picture of a proper young gentle-man," Cadbury commented when he saw Richie in his school suit. But when he looked down, he saw that the proper young gentleman was wearing high-top Day-Glo cross-trainers, laces untied, instead of shoes.

Cadbury frowned. That just wouldn't do at all.

By the time his private limousine pulled into the front driveway, Richie had changed into the boring, brown wing-tip shoes that were regulation footwear for his school. Cadbury's orders.

It took the usual forty-five minutes for the chauffeur to drive him to school. That was forty minutes to exit the Rich estate and five minutes to get to the school.

The school was a huge, ivy-covered man-sion that sat in the middle of a well-cared-for estate with an always neatly mowed lawn and freshly trimmed hedges. Not to mention the horse stables, Olympic size swimming pool, outdoor tennis court, and regulation-size running track. It was an exclusive place. A brass plate over its main entrance stated plainly:

MT. EXETER ACADEMY
"Dignity, Decorum, Dollars"

Richie stepped out of his limo with his briefcase and hurriedly climbed the few steps to the school. He was late for his first class: Intermediate Level Corporate Management.

His teacher was in the middle of giving a lecture and didn't even see him enter the classroom. Richie slid past the other students all of whom were sitting at their large mahogany executive-style desks complete with personal computers, telephones, fax machines, and Rolodexes.

"Let's move to case study number twelve," said the teacher, himself dressed in a three-piece business suit. "Your company is in dire straits. Sales are down fifty percent due to stiff price competition."

Richie was already bored by the time he reached his own desk. He looked around at the other students. Everyone looked so much older than their real ages. His mind couldn't help but wander back to the group of kids he saw playing softball at the United Tool Company presentation the day before. Unlike his classmates, those kids looked like they were having fun.

"Dividends are falling," continued the teacher. "Stockholders are screaming for accountability and demanding you step down as chairman of the board. What do you do to get the board on your side and avoid impending bankruptcy? Reynolds?"

Reynolds, a bespectacled twelve-year-old at a desk in the back, looked up from his copy of the *Wall Street Journal*. "I'll have my secretary get back to you on that," said the boy.

The teacher scowled and turned to another boy who was standing by his desk putting golf balls into a practice hole.

"Elsworth," said the teacher. "How would you get the board on your side?"

"Bribe someone," said Elsworth as he sunk another golf ball.

"Wrong," said the teacher.

Elsworth looked up. He couldn't believe he was wrong. "Bribe a lot of someone's?" he asked, trying to correct himself.

The teacher shook his head and pointed to Reggie, a boy who was standing on top of his desk and was being fitted for a new suit by his own private tailor.

"Reginald?" said the teacher.

"What would I do?" replied Reginald as if ready with an answer. "Simple. I'd float a rumor that we're the object of a takeover bid, and as soon as our stock went up, I'd sell."

"That's not only unethical, Reggie," the teacher commented. "It's illegal."

"Hey, I'm only twelve years old," shrugged Reggie. "I can't be held legally responsible for my actions."

By this time Richie had lost complete interest in the lecture and was finishing up a rough caricature of Reggie on a piece of notepaper. He slipped the drawing into his fax machine. Seconds later a copy of a boy who was clear across the room rolled out of the fax machine.

The beeps and whirrs of Richie's fax machine caught the teacher's attention. "Richie," the teacher called. "Are you and Cuthbert passing notes again?"

"No, sir," said Richie innocently.

"Then perhaps you can answer the question."

Richie thought for a moment. He wondered how his father would solve the problem.

"Um, well," he began. "Instead of firing workers, why couldn't all the board members take a pay cut?"

Richie's classmates exploded with laughter at the notion.

"Yeah, right," said Reggie Van Dough

snidely. "Like we're gonna stay rich and powerful by voting ourselves pay cuts. Good move, Chief Executive Moron."

Richie's face turned red with embarrassment as his classmates laughed at him again.

Later Richie and his classmates changed into their white fencing uniforms and headed for the gym. He was parrying with Reynolds, but Reynolds was holding a conversation with Cuthbert and Elsworth.

"Of course, long-term capital appreciation is all well and good," said Reynolds as he leaped down the marble staircase with the other boys. "But not without a sound growth strategy."

"Well, I've only got one word to say to you," shouted Elsworth from behind. He waved his foil majestically. "Plastics! What do you think, Richie old boy?"

"I think that all we ever talk about is money," replied Richie. "We should be having fun."

The boys threw Richie blank looks. They thought they were having fun. "But money is fun," said Elsworth.

"All I'm saying ... " started Richie. "Look, maybe you guys could come over this weekend. And we could just, you know ... hang out?"

"Hang out?" repeated Elsworth. He had never uttered the phrase before.

"Yeah," said Richie. "Like normal kids."

Reynolds took a step closer to Richie. He had a look of concern on his face. "You're really acting weird, Rich," he said in a serious voice. "Anyway, no can do. I promised Dad I'd go to Tokyo with him for a hostile takeover."

Richie threw a hopeful glance to Elsworth.

"Sorry," Elsworth said apologetically. "Trustees meeting."

Richie nodded with understanding, but couldn't hide his disappointment. For the rest of the day he went to his various classes distracted. He was unable to concentrate on any of his subjects. Not Stock Market

54

Trends or Special Interest Lobbying or even his favorite, Four Star Dining Etiquette. Nothing seemed fun to him anymore.

After school he sat cheerlessly in the backseat of his limousine and pined. Cadbury had just gotten off the telephone where he was scheduling Richie's after-school activities: a Latin lesson, polo instruction, a calculus lesson, and a tax-law seminar.

That's when Cadbury noticed the sad look on Richie's face.

"Something amiss, sir?" the valet asked.

"First my friends are too busy to hang out with me," replied Richie. "Now I'm too busy to hang out with me."

"Master Rich, you are being groomed for a life of great wealth and responsibility," explained Cadbury. "Certain sacrifices must be made."

Suddenly Richie's eyes brightened with an idea. "Cadbury, I'm changing my schedule," he said. Then he leaned forward to the chauffeur. "Bascomb, make a right."

The driver steered the limousine around a

corner and didn't stop until Richie told him to. By that time they were in front of the United Tool Company building. The field next to the building was filled with the workers' kids. And they were playing another game of softball, just as Richie had hoped.

If the kids wouldn't hang out with him, he decided, then he would just have to hang out with the kids.

Chapter 6

"Master Richie, no!" exclaimed Cadbury with alarm. "You can't play with those children. I must protest in the strongest terms!"

"Chill, Cadbury," said Richie as he climbed out of the limo and headed for the field. "I'll be fine."

"But they probably haven't even been vaccinated!" shouted Cadbury.

But by then Richie was hopelessly out of earshot and making his way around the mesh fence that separated the field from the street.

As soon as they saw Richie approach, the

kids stopped playing and walked up to him.

"Check it out," said a kid named Omar. He had never been this close to a rich kid before.

"I'm Richie."

"We know who you are," said another kid. It was Gloria, the team pitcher. Richie figured her to be the same age as he, twelve.

"What, no chopper?" asked Tony, another kid. He remembered the way Richie had arrived at the presentation the day before.

"Dad hardly ever lets me take the helicopter to school," Richie said.

Then Peewee, the smallest of the group, popped his head forward. "You kidding me," he said with a sarcastic laugh. "No chopper to go to school in? Man, that's rough!"

The other kids laughed. All except Gloria. She looked at Richie with suspicion.

"So what are you doing here?" she asked him.

"I was just wondering if maybe I could play with you guys?" Richie asked.

The kids looked at each other, momentarily taken aback.

"Nahhhh," they said together and headed back toward the field.

"C'mon," pleaded Richie. "Let me hit."

"Forget it," snapped Gloria walking away. "You probably couldn't hit a beach ball."

"I could hit off you," said Richie.

Gloria stopped and turned as if on a dare. "You think you're so hot?" she said in a fiery tone. "Put your money where your mouth is."

"You mean, bet?" asked Richie, surprised.

"Yeah," said Tony. "Five says she'll put you away."

"Five?" asked Gloria. "No way. How about ten?"

"Okay," agreed Richie. "Seems a little steep. Ten thousand it is."

The kids let out a stunned murmur.

"Not ten thousand," Gloria corrected Richie. "Ten dollars."

"Oh," said Richie embarrassed.

"You're on. Don't go away." Richie jogged over to Cadbury, taking off his jacket along the way.

"Sir," began Cadbury as he took Richie's jacket and neatly folded it over his arm. "I must say, I think it unseemly in the extreme for you to take these ruffians' money."

"What are you doing?" called Tony impatiently. "Asking the old guy for batting tips?"

At the words "old guy," Cadbury's eyes narrowed. "Hit a touchdown, Master Rich," he said. And with that Richie ran off to play softball.

"It's called a homerun, Cadbury." Richie yelled as he ran off toward the field. "Just watch!"

Tony tossed the softball to Gloria.

"Dust him," he told her.

"Don't worry," Gloria said reassuringly. "Mr. Fancy Pants is going down."

Richie grabbed a bat that was leaning up against the batter's cage and walked up behind the plate. He loosened his tie and rolled up his sleeves.

He eyed Gloria who was on the pitcher's mound as she wound up and fired her first pitch. It was a fast ball aimed right at Richie's head.

Richie ducked and hit the ground as the ball whizzed overhead and struck the batter's cage.

The kids laughed.

Richie got to his feet and brushed himself off, acting as if nothing had happened. His white button-down shirt was now brown with dirt.

"Put one over," Richie shouted at Gloria. "If you've got the guts."

Gloria took the challenge and tightened her lips. She wound up a second time and threw the ball. This time it was straight, right down the center of the plate.

Richie swung and hit the ball sending it high into the air and far across the outfield.

Cadbury, who had gotten out of the limo to watch Richie play, pumped the air with his fist. "Yes, Master Richie!" he shouted proudly. "Yes! Yes!" Then, realizing how unstately he looked, Cadbury lowered his arm, cleared his throat, and reservedly said, "Good show."

The group of kids were dumbfounded.

"Lucky swing, I guess," Richie said as Gloria approached him. He didn't want to rub it in. After all, how many kids get batting tips from Reggie Jackson? "So, would you guys like to come over to my house? We could — "

"Take your money and get out!" said Gloria abruptly.

"I don't want the money," said Richie.

"I said take it and leave. You don't belong with us."

"Gloria," interjected Tony. "If he said he don't want it — "

But Gloria remained silent. A silence that let Richie know he was not wanted there. He turned and walked back toward the car.

Before long, Cadbury had fallen in step behind him.

"Truly a prodigious blow, sir," Cadbury congratulated the boy.

But Richie was too upset to answer Cadbury. He took one last glance at the kids on the field. They had resumed their softball game.

Then he climbed into the limousine and slammed the door shut.

Chapter 7

That Saturday morning Ferguson made sure he got to the Riches' private airstrip early. It was his job to make sure that Mr. Rich's private jet was safe and secure.

Only this time he had to make sure that everything was not safe. He had gone over all the details with Mr. Van Dough the night before. He knew that the Riches were going to England to visit the Queen on her birthday. As usual, they would be bringing a great many gifts with them. Ferguson was to gift-wrap a bomb and plant it among the other packages. As soon as the plane was high over the Atlantic, the bomb would go off. The entire Rich family would be killed. Then Van Dough would take over Rich Industries and run things his way.

Of course, Ferguson would remain as head of security. Ferguson had just planted the gift-wrapped bomb in with the rest of the packages being loaded onto the plane when the Riches pulled up in their limousine.

Cadbury got out first and held the door open. Then Richie emerged, followed by his mother and father. He wasn't acting excited about the trip.

Mr. Rich was holding the Smellmaster.

"Richard," said Mrs. Rich. "Please tell me you aren't seriously considering giving the Queen the Smellmaster for her birthday."

"Why not, Regina," Mr. Rich asked innocently. "She'll get a kick out of it. Anything to get her mind off those children of hers, right, Richie?"

Instead of replying, Richie just shrugged and stared at the ground.

"Perk up, son," his father said. "In just a few hours you'll be enjoying tea and crumpets at Buckingham Palace."

"Whoop-ee" Richie grumbled and climbed the ramp to the jet. "I'd rather eat hot dogs at Wrigley Field."

Ferguson walked over to the Riches just as they were climbing the steps into the plane.

"Security check complete, sir," he reported. "Hope you and your family have a great time."

"Thank you, Ferguson," said Mr. Rich and went inside the aircraft. Then Ferguson quickly got into his car and drove away. He had to report back to Van Dough in a hurry.

Before she followed her husband inside, Mrs. Rich turned to Cadbury.

"Cadbury," she began. "What's bothering Richie?" She could see Richie sitting at one of the jet windows with a forlorn expression on his face.

"He tried to make friends with some children yesterday," Cadbury explained to Mrs. Rich. "It wasn't a great success."

"The poor dear," said Mrs. Rich with concern "He must be miserable."

"Might I make a suggestion, madam?"

"Anything."

"Why not let Master Richie stay here for the weekend? Young gentlemen can find the formalities of royal functions a trifle boring, whereas here I could prepare a busy schedule of distractions."

Mrs. Rich thought about the idea for a moment. It sounded good.

"Cadbury," she said. "You're a genius. I'll go tell Richie."

Mrs. Rich hurried up the steps to tell her son the good news.

Later that day Ferguson opened two tall mahogany doors and entered Mr. Van Dough's office at Rich Enterprises. Van Dough was standing in front of a huge wall fish tank, waiting. Inside the tank a group of sharks cut back and forth in the water. Van Dough got great pleasure watching the vicious and ruthless creatures. He knew their instincts were the same.

"They all got in the jet, sir," Ferguson reported. "It took off an hour ago."

Van Dough smiled. "Make me a drink, Ferguson," he ordered.

While Ferguson prepared the drink, Van Dough walked over to the window and looked out.

"Finally, my father will have his revenge," he said.

"Your father, sir?" asked Ferguson as he handed the drink to his boss.

"Forty years ago my father founded this company," Van Dough explained.

"But I thought Mr. Rich's father — " interrupted Ferguson.

"Well, yes, yes," Van Dough agreed begrudgingly. "But twenty-five years ago they parted company. Father wanted to run the business like a business. Mr. Rich, like a charity ward." Then, remembering Richie, he added distastefully, "Like father, like son."

"What did your father do then?" asked Ferguson.

"He was a businessman. He started a new business. Biochemical weapons."

"Excuse me, sir?" asked Ferguson. He could tell that Van Dough seemed embarrassed by the subject.

"Biochemical weapons!!" shouted Van Dough. "Weapons! How did he know they'd be banned? He was stuck with an enormous stockpile. He died penniless and left me nothing."

"Nothing?" asked Ferguson. "I thought you had a trust fund. Ten million dollars."

"Well, practically nothing," Van Dough said. "And look at Mr. Rich. He went on to a life of unbridled power and success. And everything he has should be mine."

Ferguson thought of the bomb he had

planted on the Riches' jet. "It looks like that's going to happen, sir," he reassured Van Dough.

"Yes," Van Dough nodded. "In a few short hours I'll be the Chairman and CEO of Rich Enterprises. And then — the Rich family vault." Van Dough took a sip of his drink and smiled. It was a cold, evil smile.

Chapter 8

That afternoon Richie sat on his balcony and stared out at the great lawn of the estate. He was feeling lonely. It was one thing to get out of spending the weekend at the Queen of England's boring birthday party. It was quite another to be home alone without any friends to play with.

Familiar footsteps walked up behind him. He didn't even bother to turn around.

"Excuse me, Master Richie, please" came Cadbury's voice. "Sensing you were at something of a loose end, I arranged for a little entertainment."

71

"I'm not really in the mood for the Vienna Boy's Choir today," replied Richie flatly.

"The choir was unavailable, sir," said Cadbury. "But I did make other arrangements."

Just then Richie saw a car winding down the road that led to the front of the house. As it got closer, Richie saw that the car was an old economy class station wagon. Unusual.

Richie watched as the car came to a stop in front of the house. Its doors opened and four kids poured out.

Richie's eyes brightened at the sight of them. It was Gloria, Omar, Tony, and Peewee, the kids from the United Tool Company field.

"Cadbury, I owe you one!" he exclaimed happily and ran downstairs to greet the kids.

Seconds later Richie, followed by Cadbury, joined the kids in the driveway. Richie could tell the kids were awestruck by their surroundings.

"Whoa," said Omar. "It ain't no house, man. It's a whole 'hood!"

"I've seen bigger," shrugged Gloria. She was trying to act unimpressed.

"Are you kidding?" asked Tony. "This place probably has its own zip code."

"Hi," said Richie as he walked up to the kids.

"Hey there, Rich-man," said Omar. "Just checking out your crib here."

"Crib?"

"I believe that's street slang for domicile, sir," explained Cadbury in a whisper. "An idiom."

"Who you callin' an idiom?" demanded Omar innocently.

Cadbury could only ignore the little boy.

"And now, if you wish, sir," announced Cadbury. "Luncheon is served."

"Hey, food" Peewee shouted happily. "I like this place!" Peewee was always in the mood for food.

Richie led the kids into the house. Cadbury waited politely. Diane Koscinski, the United Tool union rep, who Cadbury knew to be Gloria's mother, got out from the driver's side of the station wagon.

"Gee," she said to Cadbury. "I hope you didn't go to too much trouble with the food and all."

"No trouble, madam," explained Cadbury. "Just the usual."

Then Cadbury motioned gracefully toward the house and followed Diane as she climbed the stairs.

Richie motioned for the kids to follow him through the dining room and up a flight of stairs to another wing of the manor. He stopped in front of two tall doors.

Something smelled really good behind them.

"So are we gonna get some real food or what?" asked Peewee.

"Hey … it could happen," said Richie. "I think you're going to like this." He opened the doors. Behind them was a room filled with family servants dressed in McDonald's uniforms. They were standing behind a counter ready to serve two-all-beef-patties-special-sauce-lettuce-cheese-pickles-onion-on-a-sesame-seed-bun to anyone who wanted one.

"His own Mickey D's! No way!" exclaimed Omar.

The kids yelled with delight, raced to the counter and shouted their orders at the servants.

All except Gloria. "Big deal," she said, still trying to act unimpressed.

At that very moment Mrs. Rich was sitting in the cockpit of her private jet and checking the instrument panel. By now she and her husband were well on their way across the Atlantic, cruising comfortably at 30,000 feet.

Mr. Rich unhooked his seatbelt, "Some sandwiches, darling?" he asked.

That'd be great, honey," said Mrs. Rich. "But don't go sneaking any of those chocolates back there. They're for the Queen."

"Regina," said Mr. Rich as he headed out of the cockpit. "You know I'm dieting. The last thing I want is chocolates."

But as soon as Mr. Rich reached the cabin of the jet he began shaking the boxes of gifts trying to find which one might have the chocolates; after all, just one piece of chocolate couldn't hurt. After shaking several boxes he was about to give up when he noticed the Smellmaster sitting on a seat. He turned on the device and aimed it at one of the boxes.

"Pâté de foie gras," said the Smellmaster. Mr. Rich aimed it at another box.

"Seventeen-grain pearls," said the Smellmaster. Mr. Rich aimed the gun at one last box.

"Trinitrotoluene," said the Smellmaster. Mr. Rich furrowed his brow and aimed the device at the box a second time.

"Trinitrotoluene," the Smellmaster said again.

Concerned, Mr. Rich took the gift-wrapped box and showed it to his wife in the cockpit.

"Regina," he said. "There's no tag on this gift. Do you know where this is from?"

Mrs. Rich glanced at the box. "No, I don't," she said. "Anything wrong?"

"The Smellmaster says it's trinitro-toluene," said Mr. Rich. "And if I remember correctly, trinitrotoluene's the proper name for ..."

"TNT!" finished Mrs. Rich.

"Good heavens, darling!" exclaimed Mr. Rich. "It's a bomb!"

Mrs. Rich knew what she had to do. It was the only way to save them.

"Strap yourself in, Richard," she ordered. "We've got to dive!"

And with that she pulled the wheel sharply toward her until she could feel the plane dip. Then the plane spiraled downward to the waiting sea.

Chapter 9

As the plane plummeted, Mr. Rich struggled to open the nearest window. The intense cabin pressure made the window difficult to open, but not impossible. Once it was opened, he threw the package with the bomb out of the plane.

Six short seconds later the bomb exploded in midair missing the Riches' plane by only a few feet.

At that very moment Van Dough was standing in the middle of his office at Rich Industries looking at his watch. He had counted down the seconds and knew that the bomb Ferguson had planted on the Riches' plane had exploded.

He walked over to a world globe that stood in the middle of his office and looked at the very spot in which he knew the Riches' plane must have sunk.

Their bodies will never be found, he thought gleefully. And with that he left his office and went upstairs to a much bigger office. It was Mr. Rich's office.

And it was now his.

At the same time Richie was busy showing his new friends around his bedroom. His room was so big that one corner had a basketball court built in. As soon as they saw it, Omar, Tony, and Peewee grabbed a basketball and started up a game among themselves. But Gloria stayed out of the game. Instead, she chose to follow Richie across the room where he showed her his computer which was hidden in the wall. He also showed her his special modem.

"It's called the Dadlink," Richie told Gloria. "It's practically the only way I ever get to talk to my dad."

"I know what you mean," said Gloria. "My dad lives in California. If we didn't both have E-mail I'd probably never get to talk to him. He'd sure like this place, though. Must be great to have everything."

"I don't know about everything," Richie replied.

Gloria could sense the sadness in Richie's voice. She was beginning to understand why Richie had invited her and her friends to play at his house. He wasn't a spoiled rich kid at all. He just wanted to have some fun.

"So you guys wanna play or what?" said Peewee, approaching Richie and Gloria, bouncing the basketball wildly.

Richie shrugged. "Why don't we try the kid-a-pult?"

Gloria crinkled her brow. What in the world was a "kid-a-pult?" she wondered.

Richie gathered the kids together and led them outside to a yard behind the mansion where a structure that was no less than thirty feet high stood. A seat held by a long strip of pullies jutted out from the structure.

It was a giant catapult. A "kid-a-pult." Professor Keenbean was occupied adjusting the controls with one hand while holding a half-eaten liverwurst sandwich in the other.

Richie went first, climbing into the small seat. Then he reached over and let loose a nearby lever. The seat lunged into the air, flinging Richie across the yard and safely into a huge air-filled cushion.

Gloria couldn't wait to go next and hurriedly climbed into the kid-a-pult seat when it returned for its next rider.

"Way cool!" exclaimed Gloria as she came to a landing in the air cushion. She was finally showing how much fun she was having.

All the kids quickly raced to the kid-a-pult. They played on the ride for a long time, then paused for banana splits.

"That was nothing," said Richie. You guys wanna play tag?"

The kids stared at him. They were not impressed with the idea. That is, not until Richie led them to a garage containing a fleet of souped up motorbikes.

Richie wanted to play moto-tag!

The kids chased each other on the motor-bikes, doing donuts around the pond. PeeWee paused. "Man, this is the best day of my life."

"Well, the day's not over, PeeWee," Richie answered. "Come see what Dad gave me for Christmas. The kids followed Richie on their motorbikes. They stopped short at the sight of an enormous roller coaster. The kids thought they were in heaven.

"Isn't it intense?" asked Richie.

Everyone except Peewee walked up to the roller coaster.

"You don't want to ride?" Tony asked Peewee.

"I just ate," said Peewee, an expression of queasiness on his face.

"You always just ate," said Tony. Then he hopped into a seat on the roller coaster. The kids shrieked with delight as the roller coaster started to move.

Cadbury and Diane watched the children play from a distance. They had taken a stroll in the nearby garden where they had a perfect view of all the kids' activities.

"Just beautiful," Diane said, admiring the garden.

"Yes," agreed Cadbury. "My mother used to think these gardens were heaven."

"We had a garden in our old house," said Diane. "I loved it."

"I'm sure madam will have her garden again," Cadbury said reassuringly.

"Look," said Diane. "Don't call me madam. I don't like the connotation. My name is Diane."

Cadbury could sense Diane's discomfort

with the wealthy surroundings of the Rich estate. "Very well," he said. "Diane."

"So you got a first name?" Diane asked the butler. She was tired of talking about grand gardens and the like.

Cadbury lowered his eyes with embarrassment. He knew it was simply inappropriate to ask a servant for his first name.

"Herbert," he said shyly.

"Herb!" said Diane happily. To her it was a good, solid name. Much better than "Cadbury."

But Cadbury did not feel the same. "I am not a seasoning," he told Diane sharply. "It's Herbert."

Suddenly Richie and Gloria came roaring close by on their motorbikes. They were almost too close. Cadbury quickly pulled Diane out of the way. Diane clung to Cadbury. For a moment the two were close enough to embrace.

Diane kind of liked that. If Cadbury liked it, too, he didn't show it. That would not have been proper behavior for a valet.

Diane smiled with understanding.

When the rides were over, Diane gathered them all into the station wagon.

It was time to go home.

"Well, it's been a slice." Diane said to Cadbury as they stood in the driveway. "Maybe I'll see you again sometime, huh?"

"Perhaps you will," said Cadbury in a stiff tone of voice.

"When you get off the embalming fluid, gimme a call," she told Cadbury as she climbed into the car. "Herbert," she added, unable to resist.

Gloria waited before getting into the car. She wanted to say good-bye to Richie.

"Thanks for coming over," Richie told her.

"Yeah, well, it was kinda fun," said Gloria with a shrug. She didn't want to show Richie how much of a good time she had.

Richie looked down, sadly. He was hoping Gloria would have had a better time. Of all his new friends, he liked her the most.

Then Gloria let out a big smile. She had just been putting him on. "Hey, it was epic, okay?" she said cheerily. "And don't forget: baseball practice, next Wednesday, three-thirty."

"I'll be there," said Richie with a new smile on his face.

"Hey!" shouted Tony from the station wagon. "What about our hundred bucks?"

Gloria turned sharply toward Tony. "I told you to forget about that!" she yelled at him angrily.

"What hundred bucks?" asked Richie.

Tony pointed to Cadbury. "The penguin-looking dude said he'd give us a hundred bucks for coming out here and playing with you."

Richie threw Cadbury a confused, almost hurt, look. Cadbury was speechless.

Then Gloria quickly turned back to Richie.

"Hey," she said. "I said nobody has to pay us anything, okay? End of story. See ya later, Richie. We had a great time."

Gloria waited for Richie's frown to turn

back into a smile. When she was satisfied that it did, she climbed into the car. A moment later Diane started the engine. Then Richie watched as she drove his new friends down the long driveway and out of view.

When Richie turned to go back into the house he saw Cadbury talking with one of the housemaids. Cadbury looked grim.

"Cadbury, what is it?" Richie asked. He had never seen Cadbury look so dour.

"Master Richie," Cadbury began. It was as if he was searching for the right words. "It's your parents."

Then Cadbury told Richie what had happened. That the air tower at the Riches' private airport had lost all contact with Richie's parents.

Richie raced up to his room, Cadbury following close behind. Then he turned on his computer and activated its Dadlink.

"Computer," he commanded desperately. "Locate Dad!"

The computer whirred. "Data restricted,"

it said. "Enter secret password."

It was Cadbury who leaned over and punched in the secret code, SLUGGER. After a second, a holographic image of the Earth appeared on the computer screen. The image rotated as the computer searched for the location of Richie's dad.

Then the screen went dead.

"Dad not found," said the computer. "Dad not found. Dad not found."

The computer repeated itself over and over again as Richie, devastated, slumped back into his chair.

Chapter 10

That afternoon Van Dough stood at the window of his new office — Mr. Rich's old office — and sipped a glassful of champagne. He was celebrating. News of Richard Rich's disappearance was already being broadcast over all the television and radio stations. In a few hours, when the search parties found the wreckage of Mr. Rich's private plane, Van Dough's victory would be assured.

He felt like a newly crowned king.

Just then Ferguson walked into the room. He seemed nervous.

"Mr. Van Dough, sir?" Ferguson asked.

"Ferguson," began Van Dough with a devious smile. "After I plunder the Rich family vault, I was thinking about buying a country somewhere. Nothing too ostentatious. Something small, perhaps Luxembourg, Ecuador ... "

"Uh, sir," interrupted Ferguson. "There's been a slight, well, mistake. The boy ... it seems he wasn't on the plane, sir."

Van Dough swiveled around and threw a sharp stare at Ferguson. "But you said — !"

"I don't know what happened" replied Ferguson. "I saw him get on with my own eyes — and I just had them checked."

"You feculent fool!" screamed Van Dough. His face was turning blood red with anger. "You should have had your brain checked! After all my careful planning — now this!"

Van Dough took several deep breaths. He was forcing himself to become calm. He had to think clearly.

"Well, how bad can it really be?" he said, his thoughts beginning to calculate a new plan. "I've eliminated the King and Queen. The boy prince shouldn't give us any trouble at all."

Van Dough and Ferguson quickly went to work on a new plan.

For the next two days Richie and Cadbury watched every newscast in the hope that one of them would report that Mr. and Mrs. Rich had been found. But after forty-eight hours there was still no sign of the billionaire and his wife.

"They are alive, Cadbury," said Richie one night after watching another disappointing report on CNN. "I know it."

"Yes, Master Rich," said Cadbury. But his voice was grim. "And wherever they are, I'm sure they're together and happy."

At that very moment, just as he had for the last two days since his plane crashed into the middle of the Atlantic, Mr. Rich was sitting on a life raft trying to get his Dadlink to work.

But it seemed broken beyond repair.

Mrs. Rich sat next to him, her clothes just as torn and tattered as her husband's. Her eyes seemed permanently transfixed on the sky as if she were expecting to see a rescue plane at any moment.

"Richard," said Mrs. Rich. "If we ever get out of this, I'm going to soak for a week in a vat of Oil of Olay. Mrs. Rich continued, "Richard is there any more Perrier?"

"Yes, there is Perrier, but we have to ration it," Mr. Rich said. "There is no telling how long it may take for them to rescue us, because the locator-transmitter from the plane is under a mile of water," answered Mr. Rich as he twisted and prodded the circuitry in his Dadlink "And unless we see a Radio Shack soon, we can kiss off any chance of getting my Dadlink to work."

"I've thought of every employee, Richard," said Mrs. Rich.

"There's only one person ruthless enough

to put a bomb on our plane: Van Dough. When I get my hands on that bum —"

"Now, Regina, we don't know for sure —"

"Richard, wake up and smell the seaweed," she said to her husband impatiently. "You should have fired him years ago."

The Riches remained silent. It was rare that Regina reprimanded her husband.

"Darling, you know I've never fired anyone in my life. And I don't intend to start now."

But deep in his heart he knew there was no escaping the truth. Regina was right. Van Dough was probably responsible for their predicament. That made Mr. Rich angry. He had given Van Dough the chance to prove he wasn't like his father. But now Mr. Rich knew better. He also realized that Van Dough must have thought that Richie was on the plane, too. That made Mr. Rich even angrier.

Mr. Rich knew he had to survive. His son's life was in grave danger.

Chapter 11

Like all the employees of the United Tool Company, Diane Koscinski was shocked when she heard the tragic news of Mr. Rich's disappearance. But she was even more shocked when she learned that the new president of Rich Industries, a Mr. Laurence Van Dough, had ordered the United Tool Company shut down for good.

That was not the way it was supposed to be.

Like all her fellow employees, Diane went home early that day. And like many of her co-workers, she told her family she no longer had a job.

That family was Gloria.

As soon as she heard the grim news, Gloria called Richie on the private phone number he had given her.

"Closed the factory?" Richie said with shock after Gloria explained what had happened.

"It just happened," said Gloria. "My mom and everyone else got fired."

"Gloria, I had no idea they did this. You gotta believe me."

"Well, it's your dad's company," replied Gloria. "Can't you do something about it?"

Richie stood up from his desk. "Don't worry," he said with determination. "I'll do something about it."

Richie ordered Cadbury to summon the limousine. The two of them then rode to the Rich Industries office building. Richie looked up at the big glass building as he stepped out of the car. It was huge. He felt dwarfed by its size. He wondered if he really could do anything to help Gloria's mom and the others after all.

"Remember this," Cadbury said in a reassuring voice. Then he whispered something in Latin to Richie.

"What's that mean?" asked Richie.

"It means you have the power of your father within you."

"Oh," said Richie. "Kinda like 'trust the force, Luke?'"

Cadbury turned up his nose. "I suppose, sir," he said, although he had no idea what Richie was referring to.

Armed with newfound confidence, Richie entered the building and took the elevator to the top floor. He and Cadbury walked right up and introduced themselves to the new secretary who was sitting at a desk outside his father's office.

Then Richie demanded to see Laurence Van Dough.

The secretary called Mr. Van Dough on the

intercom and told him that Richie was there to see him. Richie heard Van Dough tell the secretary to bring him in. The secretary got up and led Richie and Cadbury into the office.

Van Dough walked right over to Richie and Cadbury as soon as they were brought in. He was now wearing a black armband, but it was on crooked. This led Cadbury to believe that Van Dough had slipped it on hastily, probably just before Richie had entered the room.

"Richie, Richie, Richie," Van Dough said in a saccharine tone of voice. "Let me express my heartfelt sympathies on your loss. We all loved your father and mother so much."

"What's with the armband?" Richie asked with suspicion.

"It's a sign of my personal grief on your parents' passing."

Richie looked Van Dough straight in the eyes. "My parents are alive," he said with certainty.

"I pray nightly that they are," lied Van Dough. "And we're doing all we can to coordinate search efforts."

Richie looked around the office he had visited numerous times in the past. He knew it well. By the window stood his father's huge mahogany desk. On it were the gold-framed pictures of Richie and his mother. Straight across the room was a marble fireplace. Many of his dad's awards and plaques lined its mantelpiece. Over the fireplace hung a portrait of Richie's grandfather, the founder of Rich Industries.

Everything was just as it always had been. Except for one thing.

"Why are you in my father's office?" Richie asked Van Dough pointedly.

"Because running the company can be done more efficiently from here," said Van Dough by way of explanation. "Please sit down."

Van Dough motioned for Richie to sit in a tufted leather guest chair in front of the desk. But Richie ignored Van Dough's motion. Instead, he walked around the desk and sat in his father's chair.

"I meant here," said Van Dough, again pointing to the guest chair.

"I like this chair better" replied Richie.

And as if to show solidarity with his young charge, Cadbury walked over and took position by Richie's side.

Van Dough gnawed at his lip with his teeth. He knew he had to tolerate Richie for now, otherwise his scheme might be exposed.

"Now," he said in a polite voice. "What have you come to see me about?"

"Well," began Richie. "Until my parents come back, I've taken a — what's that word, Cadbury?"

"Sabbatical," Cadbury interjected.

"I've taken a sabbatical from school," Richie continued to tell Van Dough. "You know, so I can be here and run things."

"Run things," Van Dough chuckled politely. He was trying very hard to keep his tone of voice calm and conciliatory. "Richie, the job of senior officer in a multinational corporation is, well, very demanding. The business hours go way past your bedtime. So it's best to leave the job to an adult who is experienced in these matters. Okay?"

Richie playfully swiveled around in his father's desk chair. "I don't think so," he said. "I like it here. By the way, Cadbury, how much stock do I own?"

"As your parents' sole heir," began Cadbury, "you own fifty-one percent of voting stock. A majority."

"But, you're not of legal age to exercise voting rights!" Van Dough exclaimed. He was nearly in a panic.

"But I am, sir," explained Cadbury. "And under the terms of the Rich estate, I stand in *loco parentis* and *guardian ad litem* to Master Richie and, accordingly, I give him full proxy and authority."

"So until my parents come back, I guess I'm in charge, huh?" asked Richie rhetorically. "And by the way, United Tool stays open."

This time Van Dough bit his lip so hard he actually broke the skin and drew blood. It was then that he realized that Richie was dead serious. And that he and his uppity valet had planned this whole scene. They were actually plotting against him!

Van Dough threw Richie a cold stare and left the office without saying good-bye. He now knew there was nothing more to be said. Acting polite to Richie would no longer win him any points.

The kid was obviously on to him in a big way.

Chapter 12

Word spread around the world faster than a match catches fire.

All the newspapers carried it on their front pages.

All the networks broadcast it as their lead story.

Fortune magazine came out with a special issue on the subject.

Richie Rich had taken over Rich Industries.

On his very first day as president of the company Richie was busy making sure that he was personally attending to each one of

Rich Industries' interests. When his father returned — and he was certain his father would be returning — everything would be just as it should.

That afternoon he attended the daily meeting of the chief executives of Rich Industries. Van Dough, as usual, chaired the meeting. He was explaining a strategy he had to save the company some money.

"With the losses in our manufacturing division," began Van Dough, "I'm afraid this will necessitate some employee downsizing."

Sluuurrrpppp! Richie sucked the last few drops of milk shake through his straw. The sound was so loud the executives all turned to where Richie was sitting: at the head of the table.

"Downsizing?" he asked Van Dough.

"Call it what you want, Richie," replied Van Dough. "But it's our job to cut the fat. Now let's move on to — "

"Mr. Van Dough," said Richie forcefully. "My father never fired anybody. He always said that when people are secure in their jobs, they work harder, they work happier, and they work better. I mean, if we want to cut the fat, I say we start right here."

And that's just what Richie did. He cut the salaries of each and every member of the managerial board — including his own.

As soon as Gloria Koscinski found out that her mom's job had been saved, she knew who was responsible. The very next day she and the other kids showed up at Richie's office.

It was a busy place. The secretary was taking messages from some of the most important businessmen and women in the world. Gloria and the others wondered if they would even be able to see Richie that day.

"Hey," Gloria said to the secretary. "We'd like to see Richie."

"And you are?" asked the secretary glancing up.

We're his friends." said Gloria

"Yeah," added Peewee. "And we wanna

thank him for reopening the factory."

Omar held out a baseball cap with the name "United Tool Tigers" embroidered across it.

" — and tell him that he has baseball practice. Three-thirty sharp this afternoon."

"I'm afraid Mr. Rich is much too busy to see anyone at the moment," the secretary said flatly. "But I'll be sure to tell him you all stopped by."

Before the kids could say another word, the secretary had to answer another important phone call. The kids frowned with disappointment.

Peewee walked over to a gumball machine, one that Richie had specially put in the waiting room. He dropped in a quarter and turned the handle. Suddenly the drop slot opened and hundreds of gumballs poured through the chute and onto the office floor. The secretary come running from her desk, dodging gumballs all the way.

The distraction was just what Gloria needed. She tapped her friends on their shoulders and motioned for them to follow her. When they were sure the secretary couldn't see them, they snuck into Richie's office.

Inside Richie was on the telephone.

"Marvin," he was saying. "So if Rich Candies are down twelve percent, *why* are they down twelve percent? What does research and development have to say about this?"

"Richie!" said Gloria.

Richie looked up. He was happy to see his friends. But he was even happier to see Peewee stuffing a candy bar into his mouth. It gave him an idea.

"Marvin," he said into the phone. "I'll have to get back to you. My new research and development team just walked in."

Richie hung up the phone. "Boy," he said to Gloria and the others. "Do I have a job for you."

And with that Richie and the kids held a special meeting to decide ways to improve the sale of Rich Candies.

Then Richie called a special meeting of the executives in the boardroom. The whole managerial board, including Van Dough, was present.

"And after careful consultation with my research and development team," Richie said pointing to the back of the room where Gloria, Peewee, Tony, and Omar were sitting, "I submit that we at Rich Candies have to increase our nuttiness quotient by fifteen percent, because we simply cannot allow our competition to be nuttier than we are."

The board members nodded their approval.

Van Dough could feel his stomach turn. After the meeting he stormed past his secretary and into his office where Ferguson had been waiting for him.

"That boy is a menace!" Van Dough growled. "Today he eliminated executive parking spaces. Now I have to park with the ordinary riffraff! Outrageous! I want you to put the revised plan into operation. And make sure, this time, the gloves come off."

Ferguson nodded his head with complete understanding. He and Van Dough had spent the last few days devising a plan so foolproof ... so perfect ... so devious ... they were certain that it would stop Richie Rich dead in his tracks.

Chapter 13

Richie paced back and forth in his father's office, the telephone pressed to his ear.

"Thank you, Admiral," he said to the US Navy's Chief Officer. "I appreciate your help with the search."

He hung up just as Cadbury entered the office. Cadbury could tell from Richie's expression that there was still no news of Mr. and Mrs. Rich's whereabouts.

"Cadbury," said Richie. "Maybe I'm crazy, but what if Mom and Dad don't come back?"

The very thought made Cadbury angry.

"Now you listen to me, young man," he

began. "Over a hundred years ago, my great-grandfather George was valet and butler to the fourteenth earl of Dartmouth. During the terrible war of the Crimea, the earl went missing for thirteen long months. And yet, every day, every single day of his absence, my great-grandfather ironed the earl's trousers, ran his bath, laid out his clothes, and never lost hope for a second that the earl would return."

"And the earl came back alive!" said Richie in a hopeful voice.

"No," said Cadbury glumly. "He'd been slaughtered by a marauding band of Magyars and Cossacks. However, the earl had a son, who carried on in his father's stead, becoming the first Duke of Marlborough, and he had a son. And when his son grew up, he, too, had a son, whose name, Master Richie, was Winston Churchill. So you see, if we never lose hope, anything can happen."

"So," said Richie, trying to make sense of

the story. "Keep ironing trousers."

"Exactly, sir."

"Thank you, Cadbury."

"And now," said Cadbury. "I think you could use a good stiff drink." And with that he presented Richie with a silver tray containing two large milk shakes.

"Vanilla or chocolate?" he asked.

Richie took a long, delicious sip through a straw. "Ahh. The rewards of corporate life, eh, Cadbury?"

"Yes, Master Rich," the butler replied. "But I'm afraid it's time for the board meeting."

The raft bobbed up and down on the waves of the vast ocean. The Riches sat on the raft, their clothes completely in tatters, and ate what was left of their rations.

"Well, that's it, honey," said Mr. Rich as he swallowed the last bit of food. "We're out of Perrier, the caviar's gone, and there's no more melba toast."

Mrs. Rich pulled out a bottle of champagne from the survival kit. "All we have left is this bottle of Dom Pérignon and a box of Bubblicious bubble gum, Richie's favorite."

As soon as Mrs. Rich thought of Richie, a tear formed in her eye and dropped down her round cheek. She missed her boy very much.

"He's just twelve, Richard," she said as her face clouded with worry. "He's still just a boy."

"He's grown up some, Regina," Mr. Rich said. He was trying his best to look on the hopeful side of their situation.

Mrs. Rich nodded in agreement. "And maybe we could've been there more for him. Maybe we could have given him more of our time."

Mr. Rich thought back over the years. Could Regina be right? "I was always too busy with work," he said. "What's that worth now?"

Suddenly Mrs. Rich spotted something that had just floated up alongside their raft.

"Richard, look!" she said pointing. "We're saved!"

"What?!" asked Mr. Rich. "What is it?"

"My Louis Vuitton!"

The Riches furiously paddled their raft closer to the floating suitcase. Then they reached over and yanked it aboard. Mrs. Rich opened it hurriedly. Inside were her manicure kit and dresses. And they were completely dry, untouched by the seawater.

All of a sudden Mrs. Rich began to laugh.

"Well, we're saved, Richard," Mrs. Rich said. "My manicure kit is intact and my dresses. The Versace, the Bill Blass ... "

"And look, honey. My tux," said Mr. Rich as he pulled his tuxedo out of the suitcase. "Now we can throw a dinner party."

The Riches looked all around them at the endless miles of ocean and burst out laughing at the ridiculous thought.

Then Mr. Rich caught sight of something else that was in the suitcase. Something he could really use. He pulled it out.

"My Lady Remington?" asked Mrs. Rich as

her husband examined the electric razor. "Richard, don't you think it's an odd time to start shaving your legs?"

"Regina, don't you see?" asked Mr. Rich. "This could be the very thing that saves our lives! The very thing!"

"Honey," Mrs. Rich began, "you've had way too much sun."

But Mr. Rich didn't let his wife's remark dampen his enthusiasm. On the contrary, he switched on the battery-powered razor and began humming with happiness.

He had just found their one last hope for escape.

That afternoon Richie stood at the head of the Rich Industries boardroom and addressed the managerial board. As always, Cadbury stood at his side.

"And when my father does get back," he said, "I know he'll be very happy with what we've done while he was gone, because the profits in all our divisions have continued their record-breaking rise, and in some areas, Rich Candies for one, profits are now growing at an annual rate of thirty-five percent!"

The board members applauded and nodded their approval. Cadbury, who was standing in his usual spot against the wall, smiled with pride.

Van Dough, who was seated at the farthest end of the table, shook his head in exasperation. Then he glanced at his watch just as he had been doing since the meeting began.

He had been counting the minutes until the first phase of his new plan would begin.

Just then the doors of the conference room burst open. Four men marched in, two of them in police uniforms, and made a beeline toward Cadbury.

"Are you Herbert Cadbury?" asked one of the plainclothesmen. The man showed Cadbury his police badge.

"Yes," replied Cadbury with surprise.

The second plainclothesman motioned to a uniformed policeman. The uniformed man slapped a set of handcuffs around Cadbury's wrists.

"You're under arrest," the plainclothes officer told Cadbury.

Van Dough tried to hide his smile. This was the moment for which he had been waiting.

"What is this?!" demanded Richie as he jumped to his feet.

"There must be some mistake," insisted Cadbury.

Van Dough stood up. "Officers," he said with fake concern. "You just can't burst in here. What's the meaning of this?"

"We got an anonymous tip and searched the Rich mansion," answered one of the plainclothes officers. Then he held up a sealed plastic bag. The bag was filled with electronic components.

"Look familiar?" the officer asked Cadbury accusingly. "These are bomb parts and det-onation devices found in your room. You're under arrest for the murder of Richard and Regina Rich."

116

And with that the policeman began to read Cadbury his rights.

"But I don't know what you're talking about!" insisted Cadbury as the policemen led him out of the room.

"Cadbury!" shouted Richie as he ran after his valet. But before he could get through the door, Ferguson appeared and blocked his way.

"The police have him now," said Ferguson. "Best stay here."

But Richie didn't want to stay. He wanted to run after Cadbury and help him. By now Ferguson had pulled the doors shut. Then he glanced at Van Dough. The two men gave each other a knowing look. Their plan had worked without a hitch. They had made it look as if Cadbury was responsible for the disappearance of Richie's parents.

Van Dough breathed freely for the first time in a week. He knew that with Cadbury out of the way nothing could stop him from completely taking over Rich Industries.

Chapter 14

An hour later Richie was ushered out of the Rich Industries building by Ferguson and Van Dough. A throng of reporters converged on them as soon as they appeared.

"Richie, is it true your parents were murdered?" asked one reporter as he poked a microphone in front of Richie.

"Did your butler put a bomb on the plane?" asked another reporter.

"How does it feel to be betrayed by your servant?" asked a third.

Ferguson pushed Richie past the reporters and shoved him into a waiting limousine.

Before following them Van Dough turned to face the crowd.

"We're all very saddened by this tragic turn of events," he told the reporters. "But as much as I would like to believe in Herbert Cadbury's innocence, I'm afraid that the evidence points in the other direction. We can only hope that poor Richie survives this terrible episode. And having his best interests at heart, I've petitioned the Superior Court to become the boy's legal guardian."

When Van Dough finished his statement, he turned around and got into the limousine. Inside he saw that Richie looked numb, his face without expression. Van Dough knew that the current turn of events was probably too much for the twelve-year old to take.

And that's just the way Van Dough wanted it.

At home that afternoon, Richie watched on TV as Van Dough told an interviewer how saddened he was at the shocking turn of events, and how the evidence appeared to indicate that Cadbury was indeed a murderer. Somehow, Richie wasn't at all surprised when Van Dough announced that he had requested an emergency meeting with the chief justice of the Supreme Court to discuss Richie's legal guardianship.

But the nightmare didn't end there. As dusk fell, Richie was shocked to see all the family's servants carrying suitcases and being herded into vans and driven away. Dashing back to his television, he switched on the news just in time to catch a newscaster report, "We've just gotten word that the Supreme Court has officially granted legal guardianship of Richie Rich to Laurence Van Dough, a trusted friend of the Rich family. Meanwhile, bail has been denied to accused murderer Herbert Cadbury. And, believing that Cadbury may have had accomplices, Van Dough has dismissed all the employees of the Rich family."

So that explained why the servants were leaving with suitcases, Richie thought sadly as he patted Dollar on the head. He twisted around in his chair and glanced at his computer, which he'd left on Dadlink permanently. As it had for the past week, the computer screen flashed its hopeless message: FATHER NOT FOUND.

Richie's stomach grumbled and he realized that he hadn't eaten all day. Not that he was very hungry, but he knew he had to have something.

"Come on Dollar," he said, getting up, "let's get something to eat."

They stepped into the hall outside his room and suddenly stopped. A man in a gray uniform was up on a ladder, installing a video camera high on the wall.

"What are you doing?" Richie asked the man.

"Security camera," said the man. "Mr. Van Dough's orders."

Richie became concerned. He and Dollar went downstairs. Another camera was being installed in the foyer. Off the foyer was a coat closet the size of a small room.

All the coats had been removed and a security control room, complete with closed-circuit video monitors showing various rooms of the house, was being installed. Richie felt like he was in a dream.

Ferguson was supervising the installation.

"Mr. Ferguson," Richie began to ask. "What's going on here?"

"Security system," explained Ferguson. "For your own protection."

"My protection?"

"Yes," continued Ferguson. "And until further notice I'm afraid I can't let you leave the house. After what happened to your parents, we can't take any chances."

Grrrr ... growled Dollar. Ferguson quickly yanked his hand away.

"But what about the company?" asked Richie. "The board meetings?"

"You won't be going to the office anymore, Richie," said Ferguson. "Mr. Van Dough will be running the business from now on."

Richie was stunned. In one day he had gone from running one of the most profitable companies in the world to being a prisoner in his own house. All around him Ferguson's men were installing video cameras, metal detectors, and X-ray devices.

He decided to pay a visit to Mr. Van Dough and find out for himself just what was going on.

Van Dough arrived at Rich Manor feeling like a man who had just been crowned king. It was all his now. The company, the profits, the estate. The first thing he did was call Ferguson to the living room. Then he sat in one of Mr. Rich's chairs and lit up one of Mr. Rich's cigars.

"Well, sir," said Ferguson. "Things have turned out just the way we planned, eh?"

Van Dough threw Ferguson a sharp look. It was Van Dough who had come up with the plan and he wanted Ferguson to remember that.

"Uh, just the way *you* planned, sir," said Ferguson correcting himself. "You planned."

"Not exactly," interjected Van Dough. "The vault, Ferguson. Where is the vault? They must have billions stashed away. You're head of security. Where is it?"

"That's the one thing I wasn't privy to, sir," explained Ferguson.

"What about the professor, Greenbean, Stringbean."

"Keenbean," answered Ferguson. "Claims he doesn't know."

"The disgusting fat toad," growled Van Dough.

Unbeknownst to Van Dough and Ferguson, Keenbean was snacking on a liverwurst sandwich and listening to every word they were saying. He had bugged the living room and was now in his laboratory listening in on headphones.

"And what about the butler, sir?" he heard Van Dough ask.

"The butler," replied Ferguson with a chuckle. "I've arranged it so that Mr. Cadbury will be so overcome with guilt and remorse that he's going to hang himself in his cell."

"Oh, that is luscious!" exclaimed Van Dough rapturously.

Minutes later Richie approached the living room from the outside foyer. He was determined to confront Van Dough and find out the truth. But before he could enter the room, a hand reached out and pulled him to the side.

"Mmmmuuummph!" Richie tried to call for help, but the hand covered his mouth. No matter how hard he struggled he could not break free. In another second Richie knew he would not be able to breathe.

Chapter 15

The hand released its grip from Richie's mouth. When Richie looked up, he saw that it was Professor Keenbean. He had been hiding outside the living room listening to Van Dough and Ferguson hatch their evil plan.

"Hush," a familiar voice whispered in his ear.

"To the lab!" Keenbean continued. Keenbean quickly led Richie downstairs to his laboratory where he began to tell the boy all that he had learned.

"Cadbury?" asked Richie with alarm. "They're going to kill him?"

And make it look like a suicide," added Keenbean.

"Well, we've got to do something!" exclaimed Richie. "Bust him out — "

Keenbean rummaged through his laboratory until he found a small can.

"Ah!" he exclaimed. "Here we are!"

Suddenly the can slipped out of his hands and landed on a table. A thick white gooey substance oozed out onto the table.

Curious, Richie reached forward.

"Don't touch it!" warned Keenbean.

Almost instantly the substance began to sizzle until it finally ate through the very surface of the metal table and fell to the floor below.

"I call it Hydrochloricdioxynucleocarbonium," explained Keenbean. "Okay, the name needs work. But this baby here is the ultimate corrosive. It'll eat through a Buick."

"And prison bars," said Richie, thinking quickly.

"Exactly!" agreed Keenbean.

The plan to rescue Cadbury had been hatched.

The next morning a delivery van pulled up the winding driveway of Rich Manor and came to a stop. A delivery boy with five pizza cartons jumped out and ran up the steps to the mansion's front door.

He was stopped by Nash, a hulking security man who Ferguson had assigned to stand guard in front of the house.

"Where do you think you're going?" Nash asked the delivery boy.

"Somebody called for pizzas," replied the boy.

"At eight in the morning?" asked Nash.

Just then Richie appeared in the foyer, dressed for polo.

"And where do you think you're going?" Nash asked Richie.

"It's eight o'clock," said Richie as he neared the door "Time for my polo lesson."

"Hey, listen, dude, I got a polo lesson, too," the delivery boy said. "So if you can just tell me where Mr. Van Dough is ..."

"Van Dough ordered these?" The guard turned to the delivery boy. "Okay, come right this way." He led the delivery boy inside.

As soon as Nash let the pizza boy inside, Richie made a mad dash for the pizza van and slipped into the back. He was out of sight by the time Nash turned back to face the driveway.

A moment later the delivery boy emerged from the house after having made his delivery to one of the inside guards. The boy ran to the van, closed the doors, and drove off.

An hour later the boy stopped the van in front of the city jail building. Richie hopped out of the van and gave the boy a one-hundred-dred dollar bill.

"How do I look?" asked Richie. He and the delivery boy had changed clothes. Richie was now dressed in baggy jeans and untied high-tops.

"Like you would have a hard time getting into a country club," said the delivery boy.

And with that Richie walked into the city jail building. It was filled with busy police officers. He walked up to the front desk where a desk sergeant was writing out a report on a stack of papers.

"Excuse me," said Richie. The desk sergeant ignored him. "Excuse me," he repeated.

"Whadda you want?" growled the desk sergeant.

"Please, sir," said Richie plaintively. It's my uncle. He's got very sensitive teeth."

"And who's your uncle?"

"Herbert Cadbury, sir."

"Cadbury, huh?" said the sergeant. "Lemme see that."

Richie emptied the contents of a plain paper bag out on the sergeant's desk. There was a tube of toothpaste, a toothbrush, and a greeting card. Inside the greeting card was a note that the desk sergeant could not read.

"What's this?" asked the sergeant.

"It's Latin," replied Richie. "Just a little note telling Uncle Herbie I love him and also to remind him of the importance of proper dental care."

Still suspicious, the desk sergeant opened the toothpaste tube and started to squeeze it. Richie had to act fast if he didn't want the desk sergeant to see that the tube was filled with Professor Keenbean's amazing corrosive.

"My Uncle Herbert really does have sensitive teeth," began Richie. "Did you know that he can't ice cream without feeling excruciating pain throughout his head. He can't even eat." Richie continued.

"All right, kid, all right," he interrupted Richie, not wanting to listen to any other dental stories. The desk sergeant gathered the toothpaste, brush, and card together. "He'll get his toothpaste, don't worry," the sergeant said rubbing his cheek. Richie waved good-bye and left. He had done all he could. The rest was up to Cadbury.

Chapter 16

Cadbury was trying to make the best of his incarceration. His cell was filled with an assortment of criminal types all of whom were awaiting their day in court. All were dressed in standard prison clothes and so was he. And all were seated, circled around a deck of cards. It was Cadbury's turn to deal and they were in the midst of a cutthroat game of gin-rummy.

"Herbert Cadbury!" a guard's voice called.

Cadbury walked over to the cell bars just as the guard approached and handed him the paper bag that Richie had brought.

"Here," said the guard. "Some kid brought you some toothpaste. Says you got sensitive teeth."

At that, all the cellmates broke out laughing. Cadbury's face turned red with embarrassment.

Later that day Cadbury and his cellmates were brought to the washroom for showers. All were in their underwear, including Cadbury. Even he had to admit to himself that it was most undignified.

Cadbury walked up to a sink and looked in the mirror. His face was unshaven and wan and the sight of himself in this condition mortified him. He wished that he could go home to Rich Manor where he could take his usual whirlpool bath and properly groom himself.

He forced himself not to give in to despair. No matter what the circumstances, a professional valet does not give up his dignity. He would remain as professional and immaculate as ever.

Cadbury squeezed the toothpaste Richie

had sent him onto his toothbrush. By the time he brought the toothbrush up to his lips it had already been half eaten away, until it was just a stub.

"Talk about extra-tartar control," Cadbury muttered when he saw the remains of the toothbrush. Then he noticed that there was a card inside the bag. When he opened the card, he saw that Richie had written a message in Latin inside. He translated the Latin as he read:

Life in danger. Escape now. Use toothpaste on bars — R.R.

"Oh, Master Richie, how melodramatic," Cadbury smiled to himself.

Just then a guard led a tall, heavy prisoner dressed in a leather biker's outfit into the washroom. He pointed out Cadbury to the prisoner and then left the room thinking about how he would spend all the extra money that Ferguson had paid him to see that Cadbury was "taken care of."

The prisoner grabbed a towel, rolled it up and stepped up behind Cadbury. Cadbury glanced up into the mirror. In a flash he saw the towel whip in front of his face. Then he felt it pull tight around his neck. Cadbury began to choke as the prisoner squeezed the towel tighter and tighter.

Cadbury responded quickly and without mercy. He rammed his elbow backward into his attacker's ribs. The attacker cringed as he felt one of his ribs crack. Next, Cadbury reached back and grabbed his attacker by the back of the neck. With one mighty yank he pulled the prisoner forward and rammed his head into the mirror. The mirror shattered to bits. Then Cadbury grabbed the leather-clad prisoner by the arm and flipped him over judo style. The prisoner landed flat on his back, unconscious.

"Never mess with a man with sensitive teeth," Cadbury told the unconscious prisoner as he brushed his hands together.

At the far end of the washroom was a window with bars across it. Cadbury quickly started to squeeze his toothpaste across the bars. The bars began to sizzle. Within seconds they dissolved and fell out of the window.

But Cadbury was still in his underwear. He needed clothes and he needed them fast. He ran back to the leather-dressed prisoner who was still lying unconscious on the floor, and put on his clothes. Before climbing out through the window, Cadbury caught a glimpse of himself in one of the sink mirrors. He looked like a Victorian Elvis.

It wasn't Savile Row, he thought to himself as he hoisted himself through the now unbarred window, but it would have to do.

A few minutes later Cadbury ran down the alleyway.

"Cadbury, over here!" he heard someone call. He turned to see a boy dressed in baggy jeans and Reebok high-tops pop out from behind a Dumpster. It took him a few seconds to realize that it was Richie.

"Cadbury, you're all right!" Richie exclaimed gleefully. He wrapped Cadbury in a monster hug.

And Cadbury, for the first time since Richie was born, returned the hug.

"Sir," Cadbury said, embarrassed.

"Forgive my familiarity. I was simply caught up in the moment and I didn't mean to — but Master Rich! Dear Lord! I'm away for just a day and your taste descends into the gutter."

"My taste?" Richie shrieked.

"Look at you. Pretty radical for a butler!" Richie said smiling.

Then he pulled a newspaper clipping out of his pocket. "Look at this, Cadbury," he said excitedly. "It says they found wreckage from Mom and Dad's plane! But they didn't find any bodies."

"Oh, sir," Cadbury said sadly. "I'm so sorry. I hadn't heard."

"Cadbury, no," insisted Richie. "All they found was the plane. No bodies. No life raft.

Mom and Dad are alive. I know it!"

"And the Dadlink?" asked Cadbury.

"We can't go back to the house now," said Richie. "But I know what we *can* do. Come on!"

And with that, Richie took Cadbury by the hand and led him away from the city jail. It was time for phase two of his plan.

Chapter 17

Laurence Van Dough was standing in front of the fireplace of Rich Manor when the phone call came through. It was his man at the city jail calling to tell him that Cadbury had escaped.

Van Dough was seething. He quickly summoned Ferguson. Then the two of them stormed downstairs to Professor Keenbean's laboratory.

Keenbean was just about to take a bite out of his liverwurst sandwich when the door burst open.

"We just got word that Master Richie

helped the butler escape from jail," Van Dough told the scientist.

Keenbean slapped his sandwich down triumphantly. "I knew that!" he exclaimed. "I know everything! Everything, you hear me? And what I know about you will send you both to jail!"

"Really," replied Van Dough. "Well, in that case, I'm afraid we're just going to have to kill you."

Keenbean swallowed hard. "Well, I don't know that much," he said, backing down. "Besides, who'd ever believe me anyway? I'm a loon! My own mother thinks I'm strange!"

Ferguson grabbed Keenbean by his lapels.

"Well," said Van Dough. "There is one thing I believe you do know which will be very helpful to us."

"You can forget it!" said Keenbean defiantly. "I'm not helping you. Nothing can make me talk. You hear me? Nothing!"

At those words Ferguson pulled out a switchblade and pointed it at Keenbean.

Keenbean swallowed harder. "Let me re-phrase that," he said politely. Very politely.

Mr. Rich's stomach was growling by the time he finished recalibrating his Dadlink with parts from his wife's Lady Remington razor. All of the food, except for a half-bottle of champagne, was gone.

Mrs. Rich began to wake up from a restless nap. When she opened her eyes, it was just in time to see her husband tightening the casing of the Dadlink with one of her nail files.

"Well, here goes," said Mr. Rich.

There was a short beep. Then another. And another. And another.

"It's working!" exclaimed Mrs. Rich happily.

"Let's just hope the power holds out," cautioned Mr. Rich. "And let's hope that Richie hasn't given up the search."

"Richie?" asked Mrs. Rich. "Of course he hasn't. Look, I'm going to get changed."

Mr. Rich looked perplexedly at his wife as she opened up the suitcase and pulled out a gown.

"Darling," she said, explaining. "If I'm going to be rescued, there's no way on earth I'm going to be rescued looking like this."

Mr. Rich looked at the tattered clothes his wife was wearing. He smiled. Only Regina would know the proper etiquette for being rescued at sea.

Chapter 18

The elevated train pulled into the downtown station with a loud screech. Richie, who had been looking at the subway map mounted on the inside of the car, knew that this was the stop he had been waiting for. He grabbed Cadbury and led him out of the car.

An elderly woman pulled her shopping cart to the top of the stairs when she made eye contact with Cadbury. She tightened her grip, frightened by this "thing." She quickly scurried back down the steps, her shopping cart bouncing and clanging loudly behind her, to get as far away from Cadbury as possible.

Richie and Cadbury walked the few blocks from the train station until they reached a row of apartment buildings. The buildings were old and looked as if they hadn't been whitewashed in years.

Richie looked at the apartment buzzers until he found the name he was looking for: KOSCINSKI.

He rang the bell and waited.

Then he heard an upstairs window slide open and a familiar voice question, "Who is it? Whada' you want?"

"Gloria, it's me," answered Richie.

"Richie?" replied Gloria incredulously.

Just then Diane popped her head out and looked down. She could see Richie and Cadbury. She recognized Cadbury despite his leather apparel.

"Well," she said trying to hold back a laugh. "Look who's slumming it."

"Gloria," said Richie taking a step toward

the intercom. "I need to use your computer. It's important."

A second later the buzzer rang and Richie entered the apartment building. Then he and Cadbury climbed the three flights of stairs to Gloria's apartment. She was waiting for him on the landing.

Gloria took Richie to her room and showed him the computer she used to send letters to her dad. Richie looked at the computer. It was not as sophisticated as his own, but he thought it just might work. He sat down at the desk and turned the computer on.

Richie typed out an access number on the keyboard. He was trying to contact his own computer at Rich Manor.

"Just a few more seconds and I should be in," he told Gloria.

Gloria was very impressed. "You know," she said, "I used to think you were just some spoiled rich kid, but you're really not so bad."

"Uh, thanks," said Richie shyly, not knowing exactly what to think.

"No, I mean it," Gloria insisted. "Lot's of kids, they'd have given up by now. But you —"

"That's 'cause I know my mom and dad are still alive," said Richie. "And I'm gonna find them."

Richie and Gloria smiled at each other. Richie knew that now they were more than just new friends. They were real friends.

A few feet away in the kitchen, Diane was slapping a raw piece of steak over Cadbury's black eye. He had gotten it during his escape from jail.

"Really, madam," said Cadbury. "This isn't necessary."

"And I told you," said Diane as she pressed the meat down hard. "Don't call me madam."

"Forgive me," interrupted Cadbury, "Diane."

Then Cadbury struck a pose as if he were an actor on a stage. "'Through silver woods doth the Goddess roam,'" he began to recite.

"'Her bosom the ever-welcoming hunter's home, Diana, oh, mysterious Diana — '"

"' — we give our praise to thee.'" said Diane, finishing the poem. "Lord Byron, right?"

"You know Byron?" Cadbury asked, astonished.

"Sure I do," said Diane. "I love poetry. You like hockey?"

Cadbury stared blankly at Diane.

Just then they heard the computer in the other room, and Gloria came running into the kitchen.

"Richie did it!" she exclaimed. "He's in!"

"I told you," insisted Professor Keenbean. "I don't know where the vault is!"

Keenbean was red-faced. That was because Ferguson had tied him to a chair in the laboratory and was now choking him with Keenbean's own necktie.

Van Dough watched with glee as Ferguson

tortured the scientist, trying to get the secret location of the family vault out of him.

"Oh, please," said Van Dough as he took a sip of brandy from a snifter. "You can do better than that, Professor."

"And even if I did know where it was," said Keenbean, his voice choking, "it wouldn't do you any good."

"And why, pray tell, is that?" asked Van Dough.

"Because the lock is voice-activated," explained Keenbean. "Only Mr. or Mrs. Rich can get in!"

"Unfortunately, Professor," replied Van Dough, "Mr. and Mrs. Rich have been permanently detained. So you're going to have to come up with some other way for me to get into that vault!"

Just then the phone rang. Ferguson answered it. It was the security office. Somebody was trying to access Richie's computer from the outside!

"I'll be right back!" said Ferguson as he ran

out of the laboratory toward Richie's room.

When he was gone, Van Dough decided to continue the torturing himself. He picked up Keenbean's uneaten sandwich and waved it in front of the professor's face.

"Hungry, Professor?" he asked teasingly. Keenbean's mouth watered at the sight of the sandwich. "Too bad," said Van Dough as he took the sandwich away.

"You are despicable," said Keenbean.

"Maybe so," agreed Van Dough. "But soon I'll also be very, very rich."

At that very moment Gloria, Diane and Cadbury watched as Richie punched up the Dadlink on Gloria's computer.

"Okay, Dad," Richie muttered as he typed in the request: LOCATE DAD. "Show me where you are."

The words DATA RESTRICTED flashed on Gloria's screen. ENTER SECRET PASS-WORD.

Richie quickly typed in the word SLUG-GER.

It took another long moment, but then the words ACCESS APPROVED, LOCATING DAD were sent by Richie's computer to Gloria's. Then an animated globe appeared on the screen.

Richie, Gloria, Cadbury, and Diane held their breath.

Suddenly the words DAD FOUND, flashed across the screen. Everyone cheered.

"They're alive!" exclaimed Richie.

Next, the on-screen globe began to spin. Richie knew the computer was starting to home in on the location of his parents. In a few moments Richie would know exactly where they were.

"'Dad found?'" said Ferguson as he looked at the computer screen in Richie's bedroom. Ferguson became alarmed. He realized that the Riches were quite obviously still alive. And if Richie Rich found out where they were, it would mean the end of Mr. Van Dough's plans.

But knowing that the Riches were alive could also help Mr. Van Dough, Ferguson quickly realized. Particularly when the Riches were the only two people who could gain access to the family vault …

That's when he yanked the modem from the computer, disconnecting the wires.

Chapter 19

"I've been cut off!" exclaimed Richie.

The spinning globe on Gloria's computer monitor vanished and was replaced with the words ACCESS TERMINATED.

"I can't get through," said Richie, his voice becoming panicked. "They must have pulled the modem!"

"But they're alive!" said Cadbury gleefully. "Your parents are alive!"

Richie was happy to know that his parents were still alive. But he quickly realized that Van Dough knew it as well.

"I've got to get to the Dadlink!" he told

Cadbury. He had to find his parents before Laurence Van Dough did.

Night had fallen by the time Diane pulled up behind the Rich estate. Richie, Cadbury, Gloria, Omar, Tony, and Peewee were in the car with her.

Gloria had called her friends earlier. As soon as they heard Richie was in trouble, they raced to her apartment to help.

Diane turned off the ignition and got out, followed by the others.

"I must say, Master Richie," said Cadbury, "I'm still not convinced this is such a wise idea."

"If anything goes wrong — " started Diane in a cautionary tone.

"Look," Richie said, insistently. "The Dadlink in my room is our only chance. I'm going."

"Well," sighed Cadbury. "I am wanted for attempted murder, escape, and blowing up an airplane. Breaking and entering sounds

153

right up my alley. So let's go kick some butt!"

Richie, Gloria, Diane, and all the kids stopped short and in unison all stared at Cadbury.

"Cadbury," Richie started. "I've never seen you so excited."

And at that, Richie led the way, stopping on a hill that overlooked the estate. He and the others hid behind a small cluster of bushes. From there they could see that the estate was alight with glaring floodlights. Nash, the security guard, was standing watch in front of the house.

"Okay," said Richie. "If anyone wants to turn back, now's the time to do it."

The kids glanced at each other.

"We're with you, Rich," said Peewee. This was a far cry from the way Richie's friends at school would have replied.

"All the way," added Gloria.

"You all know what to do?" Richie asked. The kids nodded. "Then let's go."

And with that, Cadbury, Richie, and the boys made sure their backpacks were secure and their walkie-talkies operating. Then they filed through the bushes toward Rich Manor.

Soon they reached a low retaining wall. Each one of the boys hoisted himself up and over it. The last to go was Peewee. He was having trouble pulling himself over the wall until Cadbury, who was just behind him, gave him a helpful shove.

Once over the fence the group broke off into two teams. Omar and Peewee headed for the gardener's shed. Cadbury and Gloria ran over to the kid-a-pult and then pushed it back toward some bushes. A moment later Omar and Peewee joined them. They were now carrying the ammo, two sacks of fertilizer.

Richie ran forward toward the house and hid behind another cluster of bushes. From where he was standing he could clearly see the front of the house. Nash was still standing guard. Only now he was opening a bag of Twinkies.

"All set?" Richie asked into his walkie-talkie.

"Eminently, sir," came Cadbury's voice.

"Okay, then," said Richie. "On me."

Back at the kid-a-pult site the other boys had placed a bag of fertilizer in the carriage and then adjusted the whole machine according to Richie's coordinates.

Richie peeked out at Nash. "Ready," he said into his walkie-talkie as Nash took a bite out of a Twinkie, "aim ... Fire!"

On Richie's command, Cadbury yanked the kid-a-pult release lever. The carriage shot upward sending the bag of fertilizer hurtling through the air, across the yard, and down toward the front porch of Rich Manor.

CRASH! The bag hit a Roman statue which fell over and broke into bits.

Nash instantly whirled around at the sound of the crash.

"We missed!" Richie said into his walkie-talkie. "Reload! Reload!" He knew the kids had to act fast or Nash would soon come after them.

At the kid-a-pult site Cadbury and Omar wasted no time reloading the carriage with the second bag of fertilizer.

"Fire two!" came Richie's voice over the walkie-talkie.

Once again Cadbury pulled the kid-a-pult lever sending the second fertilizer bag flying through the air.

The large, dark mass careened across the sky and smashed across Nash's head sending him to the ground. He was out cold!

"Direct hit!" Richie cheered.

"Tally ho!" Cadbury called as he and the kids moved toward the front of the house.

"Nash," a voice was heard. "Come in, Nash."

Everybody looked down. It was the guard's walkie-talkie. Someone was calling him from the security room.

"Report," said the voice. "Anything wrong?"

Cadbury picked up the walkie-talkie. "Yeah, dis is Nash," he said in a disguised voice. "Everything's slicker'n snot on a doorknob. Over and out."

And with that, Cadbury turned Nash's walkie-talkie off.

The kids dragged Nash's unconscious body behind some bushes. Richie reached into the guard's pocket and removed a key-code card. Peewee reached into the guard's other pocket and pulled out an unopened package of Twinkies.

Meanwhile, Omar leaned over the unconscious guard who was covered with manure. "Man, this dude stinks!"

Next, everyone scurried to a side door where Richie slipped the code card into a special slot. The door clicked open and everyone entered the house. Richie quickly led them to a dark stairway and they descended to the basement.

No sooner had they started down the

basement hall than the kids heard some strange, muffled sounds coming from Professor Keenbean's laboratory.

Richie opened the lab door. Cadbury and the other kids followed him inside. The lights were out and it was pitch-black inside. Suddenly they heard some rustling sounds.

Someone was in the room with them!

Chapter 20

Richie quickly pulled out a flashlight and shone it into the room. He aimed the flashlight beam into the laboratory and followed the unusual sounds. The further into the room he got, the louder the sounds became. Whatever it was, was just behind a table.

"Mmmm … Uhhhh … Ahhhh … " the sounds continued.

Richie and the others slowly crept toward the end of the table. Richie raised the flashlight, ready to strike whatever it was they would come upon.

"Keenbean!" he exclaimed as he took the flashlight and aimed it down. The noises had been the muffled cries of the professor, who was tied and gagged in a chair. On his chest was the last bit of his liverwurst sandwich.

Cadbury and the kids helped cut Keenbean loose while Richie yanked the tape off his face.

"YEEEOWWW!" yelled Keenbean after the tape had been removed.

"Where's Van Dough?" Richie asked Keenbean.

"He got a phone call," said the professor. "Went running out. Laughing, snickering, rubbing his hands with glee. You know, he's not a very nice person."

Richie didn't have time to discuss Van Dough's personality abnormalities.

"Keenbean, listen to me," said Richie. "Me and Cadbury have to get up to my room. We need a diversion to get past the guards. Can you do something?"

"I think I can help whip something up," replied Keenbean.

"Gloria, you go with him," Richie ordered. "Omar and Peewee, you know what to do?" The boys nodded.

"Then let's do it," said Richie.

Richie, Cadbury, Peewee, Omar, and Tony headed out of the lab. Professor Keenbean climbed a ladder and took a small box down from a shelf. Then he and Gloria left the laboratory, too.

Richie and Cadbury climbed upstairs and peeked through a door that looked out into the front foyer. Across the foyer was the stairway, the only way to Richie's room and his Dadlink. But several guards stood right in front of it.

Meanwhile, PeeWee, Tony, and Omar continued down the basement corridor until they reached a box marked VIDEO CONTROL. They immediately opened the box and began fidgeting with the wiring inside.

At the same time Keenbean and Gloria

reached an overhead pipe at the other end of the basement.

"What is this?" asked Gloria.

"What they need is a diversion," said Keenbean. Then he began to empty the powdery contents from his box into the pipe. "This is a combination laundry detergent, dishwasher soap, and bubble bath. I call it Sudsational. This is our diversion."

No sooner had Keenbean poured the powder into the pipe than the water carried it to a fountain that stood on the front lawn of the house. Within seconds the fountain was spouting mounds and mounds of suds!

A guard in the front foyer thought something looked strange. He went to the window and looked out at the front of the house.

"Sir," he called into his walkie-talkie. "There's something wrong with the front fountain."

"Then turn it off, you idiot!" Came the reply from the security office.

The guards rushed out of the house. As soon as they were gone, Richie hissed into his walkie-talkie: "Kill the cameras now!" he ordered.

Peewee and Omar reacted on cue. They plucked out two wires and crossed them.

At that moment Zullo, one of Ferguson's top security men, was watching the monitors in the security control room. Suddenly the images of Richie's bedroom, the tennis courts, and hallways popped off and were replaced by an old Three Stooges movie!

The phone rang and Zullo answered it. It was Mr. Van Dough. The same thing had happened to the TV set that he was watching in the living room.

"I have no idea what's going on, sir," said Zullo. "We could have an intruder."

Van Dough was happy to hear that. An intruder was exactly what he was expecting. An intruder named Richie Rich. And Van Dough knew exactly where Richie was headed.

"Perfect timing," Van Dough said to Zullo

over the phone. "Secure the perimeter."

Zullo did as he was ordered. He turned on his walkie-talkie and told all the security agents on the grounds to converge on the house.

At the same time, Richie and Cadbury raced across the foyer and up a staircase to the first landing. Then they scurried down the hall to Richie's bedroom.

Keenbean and Gloria met Omar, Peewee, and Tony midway down the basement corridor.

"You go on," Keenbean told the kids. "I'll just be a second."

And with that Keenbean ducked into his laboratory. The kids continued down the basement hall and out the side door. Then they raced across the estate and to the spot where Diane was waiting for them.

"We did it, Mom!" shouted Gloria. "They're in there."

"Richie … Herbert …" said Diane as she

herded the kids into the station wagon. "You're on your own."

Richie opened the door and entered his bedroom. It was dark inside, but the darkness provided good cover. Richie slipped behind his desk and activated his computer. A message flashed across the screen" DAD FOUND, DAD FOUND.

"It's still working!" exclaimed Richie. Cadbury watched anxiously. In a few moments they would know where Richie's parents were.

Next, the animated globe appeared on the screen and began to rotate. A red dot appeared on the globe. The dot grew in size until it filled the entire screen. This was followed by a pattern of crisscrossed lines and a series of longitude-latitude coordinates.

But something was strange. Richie crinkled his brow.

"Wait," he said. "This can't be right."

"What's wrong?" asked Cadbury.

"The coordinates," said Richie with confusion. "It says Mom and Dad are here. Right inside this house."

Just then the bedroom lights flashed on. Richie and Cadbury whirled around. Van Dough, Ferguson and a team of security men had entered the room.

"Well, Richie," Van Dough said sarcastically.

"Welcome home, Slugger. You were even quicker than I thought you'd be."

And with that Van Dough stepped aside and Mr. and Mrs. Rich were thrust into the room.

Chapter 21

"Mom! Dad!" exclaimed Richie.

He ran to his mother and father and hugged them tightly.

Cadbury, furious, made a move toward Van Dough. But Ferguson quickly stepped between the two and displayed a gun. Cadbury froze.

"Now, now, Herbert," said Van Dough. "Where's that famous British reserve?"

Just then a signal came over Ferguson's walkie-talkie. It was Nash.

"Sir?" said Nash. "Got 'em."

"Outstanding," Ferguson said to Nash.

"Bring 'em in." Then he threw a satisfied smile at Van Dough. Van Dough smiled back and pointed to the Riches. Ferguson grabbed Mr. and Mrs. Rich and directed them to the door. Richie, clutching his mother, went with them.

"Why are you doing this?" Mrs. Rich demanded of Van Dough.

"Yes, Laurence," began Mr. Rich. "What are you after?"

"What?" asked Van Dough. "You mean besides wealth, revenge, and a bigger office? The vault, Richard. The Rich family vault."

"That's what this is all about?" asked Mrs. Rich with astonishment.

"Yes, yes, yes!" screamed Van Dough. "The vault! Where is it?"

Since he was still tied up, Mr. Rich could only gesture toward the window with his chin. "There," he said.

Van Dough looked out the window. "Where?" he asked.

"Right there."

Van Dough ran to the window and looked out. But all he could see was Mount Richmore.

"Mount Richmore?" he asked. "Your vault's a whole mountain?"

Mr. Rich nodded.

"Oh," said Van Dough, awestruck. "You must be filthy rich."

Professor Keenbean was in his laboratory stuffing his most prized inventions into a suitcase.

"Torture me, will you," he muttered angrily. "Well, you won't be getting any of my inventions, you won't!"

But just then the lab doors burst open. The Riches and Cadbury were led in by Ferguson and Van Dough. A second later, Diane, Gloria, and the rest of the kids were herded in by Nash and Zullo.

Thinking quickly, Keenbean crouched behind a table and hid.

"Don't worry," he heard Van Dough tell the Riches. "You tell me where the vault is and no one will get hurt."

With that, Van Dough and Zullo took the Riches out of the room.

"Dad!" shouted Richie. But it was too late. The door had been slammed shut.

"Fine chief of security you turned out to be," he heard Cadbury say to Ferguson.

"Guess I won't be winning that employee of the month award, huh?" said Ferguson sarcastically.

Ferguson and Nash guided the group past the table where Keenbean was hiding. As they passed the table, Richie happened to glance down. He saw Professor Keenbean trying to stay out of sight. Keenbean and Richie winked at each other and Richie quickly looked away. He didn't want to let on that help was just a few feet away.

The group was herded up the metal staircase that led to the Subatomic Molecular Reorganizer. Richie stared at the powerful machine, recalling how it had changed the old tires, aluminum cans, food scraps, and milk cartons into a bowling ball.

"Saint Peter on a Popsicle stick,"

Keenbean muttered to himself as he watched with alarm. "They're gonna scramble their molecules!"

"Okay, all of you," said Ferguson once everyone had reached the platform. "In the bucket."

Nobody budged. They were all too frightened to move. That's when Ferguson fired his gun at the ceiling.

"Hey, let's get in the bucket!" yelled Tony jumping into the bucket. "No big deal, see? We're in the bucket."

Soon everyone followed Tony. One by one they climbed up and got inside the bucket.

From his vantage point down on the floor, Keenbean began to worry. He needed a plan. Something that would save everyone from the certain death that awaited them in the Subatomic Molecular Reorganizer.

He quickly opened his valise and riffled through it until he came across a can of Cementia and a paintbrush. Perfect.

Keenbean took the can and brush and

crawled across the floor on his hands and knees. THUMP! He hit his head under a table and bit his lips to stifle a cry of pain.

As soon as he felt better, he continued on a few more feet until he reached the metal staircase. He quickly opened the can and poured its sticky contents onto the steps and handrails. Then he spread it all over with the brush.

At the same time, at the top of the stairs Ferguson lowered the lid over the reorganizer bucket and secured it with its latch. Everyone, including Richie and Cadbury, was inside.

"Something tells me this ain't the Pirates of the Caribbean ride," Omar said nervously.

Then Ferguson followed Nash down the steps toward the reorganizer starter button.

But halfway down, Nash's feet got stuck in the glue. He couldn't move another step.

"I'm stuck!" he cried out. Even his hands stuck to the handrails.

Ferguson, who hadn't reached the sticky part of the stairs yet, instantly realized that Keenbean must have been responsible for the sticky stairwell.

"So it's the fat professor," he said. "Keenbean! I know you're in here!"

Ferguson leaped over the side of the stairwell, avoiding the sticky substance. Then he walked toward the starter control, but stopped when he saw a patch of sticky goo on the floor in front of the controls.

"Nice try, Professor," Ferguson said out loud.

Stepping around the goo, Ferguson reached up and pulled the start lever on the control box. There was a series of hums and whirrs. Then the bucket on the platform above jerked into motion and began to move toward the waiting jaws of the molecular reorganizer's mouth.

Ferguson laughed wildly. "In thirty seconds you won't recognize your little friends, Professor!" he shouted.

Professor Keenbean watched helplessly from behind a huge laundry basket. Ferguson was right. He had only thirty seconds to come up with a way to save Richie and his friends.

Chapter 22

Keenbean watched as the bucket inched its way toward the opening of the molecular reorganizer. On the floor below, Ferguson was stalking around the tables, his gun drawn.

"Come out, Professor," said Ferguson. "Don't you want to join them?"

Just then Keenbean got an idea. He reached inside the huge laundry basket that shielded him and grabbed a towel. Then he squeezed more Cementia over the towel.

"Hey!" he called out to Ferguson. "Over here!"

Ferguson whirled around at the sound of Keenbean's voice just in time to see the towel flying at him. The towel wrapped itself around Ferguson's face, sticking to his skin and covering his eyes.

BLAM! BLAM! BLAM! Ferguson fired blindly. But he missed Professor Keenbean completely. Keenbean quickly grabbed a heavy mallot from nearby. Then he crept up and bashed Ferguson over the head. Ferguson fell to the ground, unconscious.

"I'm not fat, Fergie," Keenbean said defiantly. "I'm portly." Then he pivoted around to turn off the molecular reorganizer. But as he went to move toward the control box he found he couldn't budge.

He had stepped in the patch of Cementia he had planted to stop Ferguson!

"Professor," called Richie from the bucket as they drew nearer and nearer to the reorganizer. "Cutting it kinda close, aren't you?"

"I'm stuck!" shouted Keenbean. "I can't get to the off button." But then another idea flashed into Keenbean's head. He bent down to untie his shoelaces and slip his feet out to get to the control board. But as Keenbean began to bend, he fell forward and couldn't regain his balance. He landed flat on his knees — now he was really stuck. But desperate times demand desperate acts, and Keenbean's only hope of saving Richie and his friends was one of his newest inventions. He quickly pulled his remote control from his pocket and turned it on. As soon as he did this something stirred in his open valise. Then it buzzed.

It was Robo-bee.

"Fly, my little pretty," said Keenbean. "Fly as you've never flown before!"

Keenbean pressed another button. The mechanical bee rose out of the suitcase and hovered in the air.

Keenbean frantically operated the toggle switch on his remote control, angling it toward the right. The Robo-bee flew across the room.

Keenbean glanced back at the reorganizer. The moving bucket had just about reached the mouth of the reorganizer. Its hatch was beginning to open. He could see the arms and legs of everyone inside as they struggled to keep from sliding into the deadly machine.

The Robo-bee was nearing the control box but Ferguson was quick to realize Keenbean's plan. He began to swat and swing at the Robo-bee. But as he chased the Robo-bee in circles, Keenbean jammed the toggle switch forward sending Robo-bee slamming into Ferguson's behind. Ferguson jumped with pain and tried to bend over to soothe his sore rear end. He was so off-balance that he fell into the control box and hit the power switch, stopping the molecular reorganizer.

All of sudden everything was quiet. The molecular reorganizer had been shut off. Slowly, Richie and the others climbed out through the open hatch of the bucket. One by one they leaped onto the platform until they were all out of harm's way.

Everyone sighed with relief.

Cadbury led Diane and the kids to the door.

"Diane," said Cadbury, "take the children and go to the police. Take the path through the woods we came in on."

"Herb," Diane said gently. She knew he was going to try and save the Riches from Van Dough. "Be careful."

Gloria looked around the room and noticed that someone was missing. "Where's Richie?" she asked.

Everyone looked around. Gloria was right. Richie was gone. And so was Professor Keenbean's suitcase complete with all his inventions.

Richie ran to the gym and took one of his practice swords off a rack. Then he ran to the garage and opened the door. Inside was his fleet of motorbikes. He slipped on a leather jacket and zipped it up tight. Next he opened up Professor's Keenbean's suitcase and took out a can of Stain-Away. Richie remembered how the spray hardened any substance it touched. He aimed the can at his jacket and sprayed.

As soon as his jacket felt as hard as a metal shield he threw down the spray and leaped on his motorbike. Then he revved the motor and took off toward the family vault.

Van Dough and Zullo followed Mr. and Mrs. Rich to the base of Mount Richmore. When they reached a protruding hillside beyond a wooded area, Mr. Rich reached up and yanked on a branch. A boulder rolled away to reveal the entrance to a cave.

Several minutes later they had taken a secret elevator down to the vault.

"Okay," Van Dough said to Mr. Rich. "Open it."

Mr. Rich looked at his wife. She nodded her helpless approval. Then Mr. Rich flipped open the voice scan panel.

"For access," said the computer inside the panel, "please say code words now."

"Go on," urged Van Dough.

Mr. Rich hesitated and looked into Mrs. Rich's eyes. They both cleared their throats. Then they began to sing "Side by Side" by Steven Sondheim.

"You've got to be kidding," Van Dough grumbled. "I don't believe it!"

"Access approved," said the computer. And with that, the vault door unlatched itself and opened up to reveal a wall of bars. Then the wall of bars lifted open to reveal a brick wall. Then the brick wall pulled apart to reveal a row of bookshelves filled with books. Then the bookshelves clicked open like a door. In fact, there seemed to be a never-ending row of doors and walls that protected Mr. Rich's vault.

Finally, when all the doors and walls had been raised, Van Dough found himself looking down a long tunnel. This was the moment he had been waiting for. Pushing the Riches with him along the tunnel, he eagerly made his way to the end. When he got to the end, there was a vast room. And the room held an odd assortment of baby pictures, comic books, baseball cards, finger paintings, and other childlike bric-a-brac. In short, the vault was filled with nothing but junk. Kid's junk. Family junk.

Van Dough was dumbstruck.

"Baby pictures?" he said. "Baseball cards? Model trains? What is this?"

Mr. Rich picked up a bowling trophy and looked at it fondly.

"My bowling trophy," he said to Mrs. Rich. "Remember this, darling?"

"Our first date," smiled Mrs. Rich.

"But — what is all this?" demanded Van Dough.

"Our most priceless possessions," explained Mr. Rich. "It's what you put in a vault, right?"

"But," began Van Dough with a stutter. "But where is the gold? The diamonds? The negotiable bearer bonds? The money? Where's the money?"

"In banks, where else?" said Mr. Rich. "And the stock market, real estate, and — "

Van Dough could feel his body go limp

with disappointment. "This can't be true," he said, almost in tears. "It's gotta be some joke. Are you telling me there isn't one single solitary gold bar or emerald or thousand dollar bill in this entire mountain?"

"Sorry to disappoint you, Laurence," said Mr. Rich. "That's not what we treasure."

At that, Van Dough's face burned red with rage. He turned to Zullo.

"Shoot them!" he ordered. "Shoot them now!"

Chapter 23

Zullo aimed his gun at the Riches, but hesitated. After all, he was a security guard, not a killer.

"I said shoot them!" Van Dough ordered again.

Again Zullo hesitated.

"What's the matter, Mr. Van Dough?" came a voice from down the tunnel. "Can't you do it yourself?"

Everyone whirled. Richie was standing at the vault door. And he was holding a sword.

"Richie, get out of here now!" shouted

185

Mrs. Rich. But Richie didn't seem frightened.

"It's okay, Mom," he said. "I don't think he can do it. He doesn't have the guts to shoot anyone. Do you, Van Dough?"

"You're right," admitted Van Dough. "But in this case I'll make an exception."

Then Van Dough raised his gun and fired a bullet dead center at Richie. Mrs. Rich closed her eyes and screamed. But when she opened them she saw that Richie was still standing. Not only that, he was calmly walking straight toward Van Dough.

BLAM! BLAM! BLAM! Van Dough fired again and again, each time hitting Richie dead center. But each time the bullets simply bounced off Richie's chest as if he were Superman.

Van Dough looked at Richie, his mouth agape in amazement. Richie ripped the front of his jacket off and threw it to the ground. CLANG! The jacket was as hard as metal.

Next Richie raised his sword and lunged at Van Dough and Zullo. With one fell swoop he knocked the guns out of their hands.

Mr. Rich jumped on Zullo, grabbing him from behind. Mrs. Rich grabbed a banjo and smashed it over Zullo's head. The man fell to the floor in a daze.

Van Dough was cornered. He stepped backward as Richie took a final thrust at him with the sword. Van Dough lost his balance and fell into a row of shelves. The shelves gave way burying Van Dough in a shower of falling trophies.

"We'll lock 'em in, Dad," said Richie.

"Good thinking, son," said Mr. Rich.

The Riches then ran down the tunnel.

No sooner had they left then Van Dough regained his senses and rose to his feet. Grabbing his gun from the floor, he ran down the tunnel in pursuit of the Riches.

Once they reached the outer vault door Mr. Rich turned to the voice code lock.

"Close vault door," he ordered.

"Yes, Mr. Rich," said the computer. "Have a nice day."

The vault door slowly began to close.

Van Dough hurried down the tunnel. Ahead of him the wall of books was starting to close. He squeezed by it just before it slammed shut. He raced farther down the tunnel only to see the brick wall start to slide shut. Once again he managed to leap through in the nick of time.

Outside the main vault door the Riches pressed the call button for the elevator.

Suddenly a shot rang out in the tunnel. Bullets hit the elevator door. The Riches turned around just in time to see Van Dough leaping through the main vault door right before it closed.

The Riches looked at each other. They were sitting ducks.

"I know another way out," said Mr. Rich.

And with that he led his family down an adjoining tunnel that seemed to grow steeper and steeper as they went. At the end of the tunnel was an opening, through which they could see the night sky.

Soon the Riches emerged from the tunnel. They were now atop a mountain, a mountain that Mrs. Rich recognized instantly.

"Oh, Richard," she exclaimed. "We're in your ear!"

Indeed, the three of them had emerged through the hole in the ear of the huge sculpture of Mr. Rich's head that had been carved into the side of the mountain. Farther down everyone could see the sculptures of Mrs. Rich and Richie.

BLAM! Another shot rang out and bounced off the stone earlobe of the Mr. Rich sculpture.

"Climb down that way!" said Mr. Rich pointing downward.

The Riches began to descend Mount Richmore. No sooner had they begun their descent when a sharp laser beam sliced past and hit the mountain wall behind them. They looked down to see that Ferguson had arrived. He was at the sculptors' work site at the base of the mountain and had gotten hold of one of their rock-cutting laser guns.

BLAM! PING! Ferguson fired another shot. This time the laser beam shattered the mountain wall. Bits of rock and boulder collapsed in front of the Riches, in an avalanche, blocking their path.

The Riches turned around. Only now they were face-to-face with Van Dough, who had finally emerged from the sculpted ear, his gun aimed directly at them.

For the Riches, there seemed little hope for escape.

Chapter 24

"Across the faces!" shouted Mr. Rich.

It was the only way out. A workmen's platform was hanging by some ropes directly in front of the huge sculpted heads.

Richie jumped onto the workmen's platform. Mr. and Mrs. Rich followed.

BLAM! PING! Van Dough fired a bullet at them, but missed.

"Take cover!" shouted Mr. Rich. "Behind my nose!"

The family ran to the end of the platform which just happened to end at the bridge of Mr. Rich's sculpted nose. "Take cover behind my nose!" Mr. Rich shouted. Suddenly another laser blast came from below. This was followed by another bullet shot from above. Rock dust exploded all around.

One by one the Riches leaped from the platform onto the nose. Van Dough started toward the platform after them. Richie, thinking quickly, cut the rope that held one side of the platform up. The platform broke free and swung loose, hit the side of the mountain, and dangled there, useless.

Seeing that his way was cut off, Van Dough scrambled up over the sculpted ear toward the top of the mountain.

From where he stood below, Ferguson had the Riches in the sights of the laser gun. He fired, smashing to bits the lower rim of Mr. Rich's sculpted glasses.

The force of the blast caused Mrs. Rich to lose her grip. She slid down the side of the nose.

"Riiicchhard!!!" she screamed.

"Mom!" shouted Richie with alarm.

Richie quickly grabbed his mother by the wrist before she could slide down any farther. But his other hand, which he was using to hold himself onto the glasses, was beginning to weaken.

"Dad, I can't hold on!" he shouted.

Mr. Rich reached down and grabbed Richie's hand. Now all three Riches were dangling off the side of the sculpture like a human chain.

"Hold on, Darling!" called Mr. Rich. "I'm gonna swing you into my mouth!"

Mr. Rich took a deep breath and began to heave Richie from side to side. Mrs. Rich began to swing in turn. On the first swing she missed the mouth. On the second swing she went too far. But on the third swing she kicked her legs out and got a foothold on her husband's upper lip. Now she was able to let go of Richie and climb into the mouth.

Ferguson watched from below and aimed his laser gun again. A simple shot at the upper lip of the sculpture and Mrs. Rich would be toppled by boulders.

"Now I've got you," he said to himself gleefully. Then he took aim.

"Pardon me," came a voice from behind. Ferguson spun around just in time to see Cadbury hurl a croquet ball at him. It was a direct hit to Ferguson's head.

Ferguson dropped the laser and fell to the ground.

"Smashing," said Cadbury brushing his hands together.

But suddenly Ferguson's fist came flying up and slammed across Cadbury's jaw. Cadbury fell back. Ferguson jumped on top of Cadbury. Both men rolled on the ground in a struggle, punching and blocking blows.

As they rolled, they hit the laser gun, accidentally sending deadly beams up toward the mountainside. The beams landed everywhere slicing off a bit of the nose here and altering a piece of the mouth there.

Richie and his father darted around between the laser blasts and slid down into the huge mouth where Mrs. Rich was hiding. Now all three of them crouched inside the cave-like hole.

Outside, Van Dough took one of the dangling ropes from the fallen workmen's platform and tied it around his waist. He was planning on lowering himself into the mouth of the Mr. Rich sculpture and doing away with the Riches for good.

But there were too many laser blasts shooting up from below.

Cadbury and Ferguson rolled back and forth, each man trying to get the best of the other. Cadbury sent his fist flying across Ferguson's face. Ferguson rolled backward into the laser gun. Now the gun was firing away from the mountain.

Next Ferguson grabbed Cadbury by the collar and threw him across the ground. Then Ferguson quickly reached into his pocket, pulled out a switchblade, and lunged toward Cadbury.

"Well, if you don't want to play fair," said Cadbury as he dodged Ferguson's assault and picked up the fallen laser gun. Then he ducked to one side and brought the butt of the gun down into the back of Ferguson's head. Ferguson went down with a thud. He was knocked out cold.

"Game, set and match," said Cadbury proudly.

Cadbury looked up at the mountain. He hoped that the Riches were all right, but when he looked up he saw them huddling inside the huge sculpted mouth cowering with fear. Van Dough was lowering himself toward them, his gun in his hand.

Cadbury raised the laser gun and took aim. He waited for Van Dough to make his first landing on the bridge of the sculpted glasses frame. Then he fired, sending a laser blast directly at the bridge.

Van Dough lost his footing and fell several feet to the mouth. Suddenly his rope pulled taut, yanking him to a stop. He swung back and forth right in front of the Riches.

"Help me!" Van Dough called to the Riches. "Help me! Pleeeeeeease help me!"

"Want to give him a hand, Mom?" asked Richie.

"Gladly," said Mrs. Rich. And with that Mrs. Rich pulled her arm back and swung a punch directly into Van Dough's face. Van Dough went swinging wildly like a tetherball.

"Dad," began Richie, "I know what company policy is and I know how you feel about firing people, but — "

"Well, Richie," interrupted Mr. Rich, "in this case I think we can make an exception. Why don't you do the honors?"

"Mr. Van Dough," he said to the dazed man who was swinging back and forth in front of him, "you're fired!"

Richie smiled. It was over. His parents were alive and Van Dough would soon be behind bars. Now he would be able to get back to a normal life. At least, as normal a life as a billionaire twelve-year-old boy could have.

Chapter 25

By the following week everything had returned to normal. Mr. Rich had resumed control of Rich Industries and Van Dough, Ferguson, and the others were safely behind bars.

By the weekend Mr. and Mrs. Rich were standing behind the lines of the brand-new baseball stadium they had built for Richie. They built it right in their own backyard.

Richie was up at bat wearing a "United Tool Tiger" baseball uniform. Tony was on third, Omar was on second, and Gloria was on first. Professor Keenbean was umping behind home plate. And Cadbury was on the sidelines in a coaching outfit.

The visiting team's pitcher threw the ball and Richie swung, hitting a fly ball out of the park. Richie threw the bat down and took off around the bases following Tony, Omar, and Gloria home.

Mr. and Mrs. Rich jumped up and cheered. So did Diane, who had been standing next to them. She ran over to Cadbury and kissed him on the cheek.

"Not bad, Coach," she told the butler. Cadbury's face turned red.

"Madam," returned Cadbury, "not bad yourself."

"Don't call me — " started Diane. But Cadbury cut her short with a deep kiss on the lips.

Richie and his friends watched Cadbury and Diane. Big smiles were on their faces.

"Regina," Mr. Rich said warmly when he saw how happy Richie looked. "Now our son is the richest boy in the world. He has friends!"